Everyman, I will go with thee,
and be thy guide

William Shakespeare

THE SONNETS
AND
A LOVER'S COMPLAINT

Edited by
MARTIN DODSWORTH
Royal Holloway, University of London

EVERYMAN
J. M. DENT · LONDON
CHARLES E. TUTTLE
VERMONT

Introduction and other critical apparatus © J. M. Dent 1995

The Sonnets first published in Everyman in 1976
Reprinted 1981, 1985, 1988
Reissued 1991
Reprinted 1992
This edition with *A Lover's Complaint* first published
in Everyman in 1995

J. M. Dent
Orion Publishing Group
Orion House
5 Upper St Martin's Lane
London WC2H 9EA
and
Charles E. Tuttle Co. Inc.
28 South Main Street
Rutland, Vermont 05701, USA

Typeset by CentraCet Ltd, Cambridge
Printed in Great Britain by
The Guernsey Press Co. Ltd, Guernsey, C. I.

British Library Cataloguing-in-Publication Data is
available upon request.

ISBN 0 460 87516 7

CONTENTS

NOTE ON THE AUTHOR AND EDITOR

WILLIAM SHAKESPEARE is held to have been born on St George's day, 23 April 1564. The eldest son of a prosperous glove-maker in Stratford-upon-Avon, he was probably educated at the town's grammar school.

Tradition holds that between 1585 and 1592, Shakespeare first became a schoolteacher and then set off for London. By 1595 he was a leading member of the Lord Chamberlain's Men, helping to direct their business affairs, as well as being a playwright and actor. In 1598 he became a part-owner of the company, which was the most distinguished of its age. However, he maintained his contacts with Stratford, and his family seem to have remained there.

From about 1610 he seems to have grown increasingly involved in the town's affairs, suggesting a withdrawal from London. He died on 23 April 1616, in his 53rd year, and was buried at Holy Trinity Church two days later.

MARTIN DODSWORTH is Professor of English at Royal Holloway, University of London. He is the author of *Hamlet Closely Observed* (1985) and editor of *The Survival of Poetry* (1970), *English Economis'd* (1989) and *The Penguin History of Literature* Vol. 7: *The Twentieth Century* (1994). He has been Chairman and President of The English Association. For many years he reviewed contemporary poetry for *The Guardian*.

CHRONOLOGY OF SHAKESPEARE'S LIFE

Year[1]	Age	Life
1564		Shakespeare baptized 26 April at Stratford-upon-Avon
1582	18	Marries Anne Hathaway
1583	19	Daughter, Susanna, born
1585	21	Twin son and daughter, Hamnet and Judith, born
1590–1	26	*The Two Gentlemen of Verona* & *The Taming of the Shrew*
1591	27	*2 & 3 Henry VI*
1592	28	*Titus Andronicus* & *1 Henry VI*
1592–3		*Richard III*
1593	29	*Venus and Adonis* published
1594	30	*The Comedy of Errors*. *The Rape of Lucrece* published
1594–5		*Love's Labour's Lost*
1595	31	*A Midsummer Night's Dream, Romeo and Juliet*, & *Richard II*. An established member of Lord Chamberlain's Men
1596	32	*King John*. Hamnet dies
1596–7		*The Merchant of Venice* & *1 Henry IV*
1597	33	Buys New Place in Stratford The Lord Chamberlain's Men's lease to play at the Theatre expires; until 1599 they play mainly at the Curtain

[1] It is rarely possible to be certain about the dates at which plays of this period were written. For Shakespeare's plays, this chronology follows the dates preferred by Wells and Taylor, the editors of the Oxford Shakespeare. Publication dates are given for poetry and books.

CHRONOLOGY OF HIS TIMES

Year	Artistic Events	Historical Events
1565–7	Golding, Ovid's *Metamorphoses*, tr.	Elizabeth I reigning
1574	*A Mirror for Magistrates* (3rd ed.)	
1576	London's first playhouse built	
1578	John Lyly, *Euphues*	
1579	North, Plutarch's *Lives*, tr. Spenser, *Shepheardes Calender*	
1587	Marlowe, *1 Tamburlaine* Holinshed's *Chronicles* (2nd ed.)	Mary Queen of Scots executed Defeat of Spanish Armada
1589	Kyd, *Spanish Tragedy* Marlowe, *Jew of Malta*	Civil war in France
1590	Spenser, *Faerie Queene*, Bks I–III	
1591	Sidney, *Astrophil and Stella*	Proclamation against Jesuits
1592	Marlowe, *Dr Faustus* & *Edward II*	Scottish witchcraft trials Plague closes theatres from June
1593	Marlowe killed	
1594	Nashe, *Unfortunate Traveller*	Theatres reopen in summer
1594–6		Extreme food shortages
1595	Sidney, *An Apologie for Poetry*	Riots in London
1596		Calais captured by Spanish Cádiz expedition
1597	Bacon's *Essays*	

Year	Age	Life
1597–8		*The Merry Wives of Windsor* & *2 Henry IV*
1598	34	*Much Ado About Nothing*
1598–9		*Henry V*
1599	35	*Julius Caesar*. One of syndicate responsible for building the Globe in Southwark, where the Lord Chamberlain's Men now play
1599–1600		*As You Like It*
1600–1		*Hamlet*
1601	37	*Twelfth Night*. His father is buried in Stratford
1602	38	*Troilus and Cressida*. Invests £320 in land near Stratford[2]
1603	39	*Measure for Measure*. The Lord Chamberlain's Men become the King's Men. They play at court more than all the other companies combined
1603–4		*Othello*
c.1604	40	Shakespeare sues Philip Rogers of Stratford for debt
1604–5		*All's Well that Ends Well*
1605	41	*Timon of Athens*. Invests £440 in Stratford tithes
1605–6		*King Lear*
1606	42	*Macbeth* & *Antony and Cleopatra*
1607	43	*Pericles*. Susanna marries the physician John Hall in Stratford
1608	44	*Coriolanus*. The King's Men lease Blackfriars, an indoor theatre. His only grandchild is born. His mother dies
1609	45	*The Winter's Tale*. 'Sonnets' and 'A Lover's Complaint' published
1610	46	*Cymbeline*
1611	47	*The Tempest*
1613	49	*Henry VIII*. Buys house in London for £140
1613–14		*The Two Noble Kinsmen*
1616	52	Judith marries Thomas Quiney, a vintner, in Stratford. On 23 April he dies, and is buried two days later
1623	59	Publication of the First Folio. His wife dies in August

[2] A schoolmaster would earn around £20 a year at this time.

Year	Artistic Events	Historical Events
1598	Marlowe and Chapman, *Hero and Leander* Jonson, *Every Man in his Humour*	Rebellion in Ireland
1599	Children's companies begin playing Thomas Dekker's *Shoemaker's Holiday*	Essex fails in Ireland
1601	'War of the Theatres' Jonson, *Poetaster*	Essex rebels and is executed
1602		Tyrone defeated in Ireland
1603	Florio, Montaigne's *Essays*, tr.	Elizabeth I dies, James I accedes Raleigh found guilty of treason
1604	Marston, *The Malcontent*	Peace with Spain
1605	Bacon's *Advancement of Learning*	Gunpowder plot
1606	Jonson's *Volpone*	
1607	Tourneur's *The Revenger's Tragedy*, published	Virginia colonized Enclosure riots
1609		Oath of allegiance Truce in Netherlands
1610	Jonson, *Alchemist*	
1611	Authorized Version of the Bible Donne, *Anatomy of the World*	
1612	Webster, *White Devil*	Prince Henry dies
1613	Webster, *Duchess of Malfi*	Princess Elizabeth marries
1614	Jonson, *Bartholomew Fair*	
1616	Folio edition of Jonson's plays	

Biographical note and chronology compiled by John Lee, University of Bristol, 1993.

INTRODUCTION

Outside his plays, so far as we know, Shakespeare wrote little poetry. He published two longish poems, *Venus and Adonis* and *Lucrece* in the early 1590s when he was just coming into his thirties, and contributed a weird and wonderful poem 'The Phoenix and The Turtle' to a miscellaneous collection called *Love's Martyr* which was published in 1600, and that, apart from the sonnets and 'A Lover's Complaint', is just about the sum of it.

The sonnets were published with their companion piece in 1609 when Shakespeare's career was moving into its final stage. His last tragedy, *Coriolanus*, was probably performed the year before, in 1608. Ahead of him lay the romances, among them *Cymbeline*, perhaps *The Winter's Tale* and *The Tempest*. Shakespeare still had life in him as a dramatist, even if he was actually not to live much longer (he died in April 1616).

These are facts. There is plenty that we do not know or understand about this 1609 publication. When were the poems written? What is the meaning of the book's dedication? Is 'A Lover's Complaint' really Shakespeare's? What, if anything, did Shakespeare have to do with the appearance of the book? It is important to try to answer these questions if we want to understand the significance of the sonnets and the 'Complaint' in the context of Shakespeare's work as a whole.

It is even more important, of course, to seize the much simpler fact that the sonnets and 'A Lover's Complaint' are in any case special in the canon of Shakespeare's work. The long poems, *Venus and Adonis* and *Lucrece*, are formal rhetorical exercises, one on a mythological, the other on an ancient historical theme. The sonnets are the only poems in which a truly personal tone appears. That is their distinction.

These poems put us in touch with a human voice, invite us to an apparent intimacy with Shakespeare himself. If that is a distinction, it is also a penalty. The sonnets have been read time and again for clues about Shakespeare's life, attempts to link him with this man and that, to pin him down biographically in the shadows of four hundred years ago, and, seeing the nature of Shakespeare's achievement elsewhere, one understands this tendency to turn the sonnets into data for biography. Yet it is wrong. For the personal tone of the poems itself is their greatest achievement, one so remarkable that only the greatest of English poets could have been responsible for it. How the sonnets and 'A Lover's Complaint' came to be written and published and what they meant in Shakespeare's personal life are subjects for infinite speculation, but their remarkable quality as poetry seems now, despite the vagaries of criticism in the past, to be beyond question.

With the sort of proviso all this implies, it is reasonable to want to know as much as we can about the sonnets. Some speculations will prove to be more profitable than others. Of course, we would like to know *when* these poems were written in Shakespeare's career, for example, but this is one of the places where speculation is weakest.

We know nothing about the date of 'A Lover's Complaint'. It appears at the conclusion of the sonnets unsignalled by any reference to it on the title page. There is no contents page in the 1609 volume so the reader is given no warning that the poem is there at the end of the book. It appears as a surprise – or a bonus. It is not referred to by Shakespeare's contemporaries. We have, thus, nothing but the author's name on the cover of the 1609 volume, the poem's compatibility with the sonnets and its occasional likenesses to other passages in Shakespeare (some of which have been teased out by Professor Kenneth Muir and others by John Kerrigan) to assure us that it is Shakespeare's at all, let alone to date it.

We are in a slightly better position as far as the sonnets are concerned, however. In 1598 one Francis Meres in an odd book called *Palladis Tamia* mentions some of Shakespeare's plays and also 'his sugred Sonnets among his private friends'. He might have been referring to the sonnets later printed in 1609, but he might not. He could have been talking either about other sonnets that have not survived or about other poems, for example songs that had not yet found a place in the plays, the word 'sonnet' not having a very precise meaning in 1598. If we think it possible to describe some of the sonnets we have as 'sugred' (and I suppose some of those in the opening group 1–17 could be) then Meres could have been referring to them.

In any case, in the following year two of the sonnets found their way into print, numbers 138 and 144, which appear in a collection of poems entitled *The Passionate Pilgrim* and described as being 'By W. Shakespeare'. Most of the poems were certainly not by Shakespeare – that was just a publisher's come-on – but the two sonnets are joined by three pieces taken from *Love's Labour's Lost*; the publication was the work of an unscrupulous printer who had presumably caught the two sonnets as they circulated among the author's 'private friends'.

If two of the sonnets were written in 1599, it is possible that all the sonnets had been written by then, but it does not follow that this is so. The sonnets fall into three distinct groups. The first consists of Sonnets 1–17, intended to persuade a young man of good birth and good looks to marry. The second group is by far the largest and consists of Sonnets 18–126 which celebrate the varying fortunes of the poet's friendship with a young man, presumably the same as the first group is aimed at. The sonnets conclude with a more heterogeneous set which deals largely with the poet's relations with his difficult dark-haired mistress and finishes with a couple of mythological fancies about Cupid and his torch. Apart from Sonnet 129 this last group is, though interesting, much inferior to the rest, a weakness that suggests it could be earlier work. The two sonnets printed by Jaggard come from this group; it is therefore possible that in 1599 Shakespeare still had to write the bulk of the collection.

It is also possible that, even if he had written most or all of them by 1599 or so, he nevertheless continued to work on them. The plays show that Shakespeare was in the habit of adding new passages and removing old ones as plays underwent perform-ance – at least, this seems the best way to explain differences between the early versions of *Hamlet*, *King Lear* and *Othello*. It is therefore plausible that he should have also gone back to poems he had written a few years earlier and altered them. This could have happened to the sonnets at any time between their first composition and the appearance of the printed book in 1609. In Shakespeare's day and for some time thereafter it was customary to compile collections of especially valued poems in manuscript. More than twenty of these collections contain versions of Shakespeare's sonnets, sometimes in a form obviously derived from the printed book (they are all dated later than 1609), sometimes with significant variations. These variations can be explained if we assume them to be derived ultimately from the copies that circulated among Shakespeare's 'private friends'. They would then reflect earlier versions of sonnets subsequently revised.

If we want to date Shakespeare's sonnets, then, we have a hard task. Some of them were written by 1599. Some could have been written quite a bit earlier than that; but they could equally well be the work of later years or at least bear the marks of revision. Because of this wide span of time in which the sonnets could have been written resemblances to verse in plays of the early 1590s or those of the 1600s are equally plausible. Speculation inclines me to think that the bulk of the sonnets were written later than 1599 rather than earlier: the difficult relationship with a young man of plausible or commandingly handsome appearance parallels what we find in *Measure for Measure* and *All's Well that Ends Well*, plays of the early years of the seventeenth century, and stylistically there seems to be compatibility. But the reader, given the wide range of possibility, need not take this speculation too seriously.

The mysterious nature of 'A Lover's Complaint' has already been described. It is hardly surprising that a book printed in 1609 should lack a table of contents, though one might have expected some mention of a poem as sizeable as 'A Lover's Complaint' on the title page. Editors on the whole have taken against it, perhaps because it is rather rough, employing, for example, a great many words that occur nowhere else or very rarely, creating a difficulty compounded by sometimes rather free sentence structure. But their chief reason for a dislike that has usually been expressed as reluctance to consider the poem as Shakespeare's at all has been their belief that the sonnets were printed without the authority of their author.

This belief arose from a distrust of the printer of the sonnets, a certain T. T., or Thomas Thorpe, a distrust which editors made explicit, and perhaps also from an unwillingness to believe that Shakespeare *could* have authorized the publication of a document as personal as the sonnets, an unwillingness to which they gave no direct expression. The case against Thorpe lay chiefly on the basis of his having made arrangements with two different booksellers to sell the book for him, so that some copies of the first edition say that the book is to be sold by William Aspley whilst others direct the reader for more copies to 'John Wright, dwelling at Christ Church gate'. This was thought to be a tactic on Thorpe's part to make suppression of the book by an angered author difficult, but it could just as well be prudent business management, spreading risk along with profit among several people. Thorpe himself has been shown in recent studies by Leona Rostenberg and Katherine Duncan-Jones to have been a careful and responsible printer with particularly good contacts in the theatrical world, printing work by Chapman, Jonson, Marlowe and Marston. Jonson's connection with him is especially telling in his favour because Jonson was hard to please where the printing of his work was concerned and Jonson was a friend of Shakespeare's. (Did Shakespeare die after a drinking-bout with Jonson and the sonnet-writer Drayton? We shall never know.) Given this background, it hardly seems likely that Thorpe would have stepped out of line by printing an unauthorized text of Shakespeare's poems, particularly as he had cleared the books in the usual way with the Stationers' Company to secure copyright. If Thorpe was an honest man, then two things follow: that Shakespeare wanted the sonnets to be published and that 'A Lover's Complaint' is by him and properly associated with them. And why not? The sonnets are a great achievement in poetry and doubtless reflect a relationship of considerable complexity and significance in Shakespeare's life. Why should he not want them published? And why should not 'A Lover's Complaint' accompany them? It is a story of love betrayed which is well in harmony with later poems in the central sequence of sonnets. Furthermore it was not unusual for such sonnet-sequences to conclude with a related longer poem in another form (as, again, Katherine Duncan-Jones has argued). Samuel Daniel's *Delia* (1592), Thomas Lodge's *Phillis* (1593) and Edmund Spenser's *Amoretti* (1595) all follow this pattern. In the absence of evidence to the contrary, 'A Lover's Complaint' must be regarded as Shakespearean.

The likelihood that Shakespeare himself was behind the publication of the sonnets also affects the way we may look at the order in which they are printed. The notion that there was something underhand about the way in which the printer had obtained the copy for his edition of the sonnets was useful to all those people who wanted to read them as documents in Shakespeare's life. It gave them a licence to shift poems out of their original order so that they might tell a 'better' story. After all, it was plausible that if the sonnets had arrived in Thorpe's hands by some devious and illegitimate route they should also have come in some disarray. The very personal tone of the writing encouraged the quest for a 'better' ordering of the poems, one that would at last reveal the 'truth' about Shakespeare's relations with the young man. Such attempts to re-order the sonnets continue to this day. It is striking that not one of these many re-orderings of the poems has stuck as a point of reference for interested readers. And in fact the order of the sonnets as they were printed in 1609 is not more or less coherent than that of the sonnets in Daniel's *Delia* or Drayton's *Idea*. It was the exception, not the rule, for a sonnet-sequence to tell a coherent story as did Sidney's *Astrophil and Stella* and Spenser's *Amoretti*.

It was the seekers for biographical 'truth' who also made such a fuss about the dedication of the sonnets. There certainly is room for speculation here, though whether it is helpful may be doubted. Thorpe attached a dedication to his edition of the sonnets, set out in capitals and made to suggest a Roman inscription, thus adding dignity to his small but powerful volume:

TO. THE. ONLIE. BEGETTER. OF.

THESE. INSVING. SONNETS.

M^r. W. H. ALL. HAPPINESSE.

AND. THAT. ETERNITIE.

PROMISED.

BY.

OVR. EVER-LIVING. POET.

WISHETH.

THE. WELL-WISHING.

ADVENTVRER. IN.

SETTING.

FORTH.

T. T.

It is the initials 'W. H.' that have caused the trouble. Could they refer to the young man? If they do, then we have a clue to his name. He could be William Herbert, third Earl of Pembroke (1580–1630), or, if we allow that for some reason (discretion?) letters have been reversed, to Henry Wriothesley, third Earl of Southampton (1573–1624), to whom Shakespeare had dedicated both *Venus and Adonis* and *Lucrece*. But a lot depends on that 'if'. The characterization of Mr W. H. as 'begetter' of the sonnets harmonizes with the opening sequence of poems persuading the young man to marry and so to perpetuate his beauty. To suggest that the begetting he has accomplished is that of these remarkable sonnets would be a neat, but worryingly cheeky, compliment, as coming from a printer to a man of high birth. Still, in wishing him the eternity promised by the poet, Thorpe is not necessarily saying that his dedicatee is also the subject of the sonnets. It has been argued that 'begetter' does not mean 'inspiration' for the writing of these sonnets but 'procurer' of them, that is, the go-between between Thorpe and Shakespeare who clinched the deal or, if we wish to stick with the notion that Thorpe's publication was unauthorized, the man who stole the sonnets from the papers of the author's 'private friends'. It is not easy, therefore, to determine either who Mr W. H. was or what his relation to Shakespeare might have been. Even to say that I incline to think that Mr W. H. was indeed Shakespeare's young man gets us very little distance on the way to linking the sonnets with William Herbert or Henry Wriothesley.

The intimacy, then, of Shakespeare's sonnets is of a very particular kind. The reader is largely in the situation of an overhearer. There is a conversation taking place between Shakespeare and his young man, but we are not in a position either to hear what the young man says or to see who he is. We are at once inside the conversation, caught up in its intensity of feeling and its exploration of relationship, and outside, looking in. This is not the effect of other sonnet-sequences.

For Shakespeare's sonnets are the product of a very particular fashion in Elizabethan poetry for the sonnet-sequences. The sonnet itself had been introduced to England in the early sixteenth century by Sir Thomas Wyatt; several of his sonnets translate from the Italian of Petrarch (1304–74) and the form itself goes back to the Italian thirteenth century. Petrarch's sonnets concern themselves with his devotion to the virtuous and beautiful woman Laura and gave rise to collections of sonnets by other poets all over Europe dedicated to other women (or other subjects than love). The first collection of English sonnets dedicated to a single woman (and, in this case, as in a few others, mingled with lyric poems in other forms) was John Soowthern's *Pandora* of 1584, a justly rare volume. It was Sir Philip Sidney's sequence *Astrophil and Stella* (1591) which really set the English off. It is a magnificent work of art which tells the story of unsuccessful wooing in 108 sonnets and eleven intermingled songs, and gave rise to sequences by Daniel, Spenser, Drayton and many others, the best of which are still worth reading today. Shakespeare's sonnets come very much at the end of this burst of sequences in 1609. Between 1591, when Sidney's *Astrophil and Stella* came out, and 1600, sixteen sequences were published. Between 1600 and 1609 there was only one, and that was Scottish (Sir William Alexander's *Aurora*, 1604) and probably written at least ten years earlier.

Shakespeare's sonnet-sequence comes late on the scene. One of the reasons for thinking that its maturity of expression owes something to revision is this very fact: that its genesis ought to be somewhere in the mid-1590s, but that in effect it is so unlike the sonnets of this decade. For essentially what these earlier poems do is put love on display. This is especially true of Sidney whose poetry thrived on artifice, using it to put an edge on what might otherwise seem insipid. His Sonnet 59 in *Astrophil and Stella* is on a conventional theme, comparing his own lot with that of Stella's lap dog: 'Dear, why make you more of a dog than me?' There are other such sonnets in French and Italian; Sidney makes his stand out by the heavy use of monosyllables so that he sounds both stereotypical like a stereotypical blunt Englishman and also like a man who could be keeping his words in check. His sonnet is, as usual with him, tightly controlled by rhyme. The first eight lines form a unit (commonly called the octave) which rhymes on two sounds only: *me, love, move, be, he, prove, glove, thee*. The sonnet is then made up of a quatrain followed by a couplet: *clips, spite, lips, delight, wit, it*. But Sidney cunningly suggests that his feeling is too strong to be contained within the form he has decreed it. His last statement in the sonnet is too much to be expressed merely in the last two lines; it demands three, so breaking the symmetry of the poem. Furthermore the sentence itself loses poise, ending in the dribbling monosyllable *it*, stopping and starting in its course, straddling the line-break with an awkward but irrepressible parenthesis:

> Alas, if you grant only such delight
> To witless things, then Love, I hope (since wit
> Becomes a clog) will soon ease me of it.

The poem declares, puts on show, the poet's subjection to love and his resentment of it in a display of feeling restrained and yet uncurbed. It is brilliant and it is theatrical.

Since Shakespeare is a dramatist, you might expect him to write in this mode also. But he does not. His sonnets are more elusive in quality, do not declare themselves so readily. The Shakespearean sonnet is not so weighty as Sidney's, though it is infinitely more impassioned and subtle. Shakespeare does not mark off the octave from the sestet as clearly as does Sidney; his sonnet simply consists of three quatrains and a couplet. The pointed imbalance of eight lines against six which Sidney uses with assurance is merely a possibility in Shakespeare. His thought often develops itself in quatrain upon quatrain in an apparently unrehearsed, expansive thrust, often brought short by the final couplet which seems by summing up to turn its back on what has already been said. The result is that the reader feels that entry to a personal world has been permitted and then, abruptly, the permission has been withdrawn. Each sonnet seems to begin again something that its predecessor has already attempted, but each sonnet is coloured by the emotions of the moment and these change rapidly.

> When to the sessions of sweet silent thought
> I summon up remembrance of things past,
> I sigh the lack of many a thing I sought . . .
>
> (Sonnet 30)

The court-room in which the sessions of memory are held is sweet and silent but soon invaded by the sighs of regret and of a desire that still seeks satisfaction. The lines promote a harmony of sound which is unsettled by what it reveals. That seems typical of Shakespeare's poetic movement, of the expansive, exploratory nature of thought as it figures in the sonnets. Sonnet 30 overflows into the next, as so many of these poems do. It ends with the thought that to think of his friend makes up for all loss and sorrow and leads to the first lines of Sonnet 31:

> Thy bosom is endeared with all hearts
> Which I by lacking have supposed dead . . .

'In you, I love all the things I have loved before in other people' – that is a weak way of putting what Shakespeare says here. It would be more accurate to say that in his friend he loves all the people he has loved and lost before in his life. It is an odd thought because it praises the friend but also threatens to diminish him as merely the sum of others' parts. But then the thought changes again as the sonnet moves on, changes to something fantastic and compelling:

> Thou art the grave where buried love doth live,
> Hung with the trophies of my lovers gone . . .

The lines balance death against life in the strangest of ways. They are comparable with the lines in *The Winter's Tale* where Perdita also brings together love and the grave. She is lamenting the lack of flowers with which to adorn her lover Florizel:

> O, these I lack,
> To make you garlands of, and, my sweet friend,
> To strew him o'er and o'er.
>
> *Florizel*: What? Like a corse?
> *Perdita*: No, like a bank, for love to lie and play on;
> Not like a corse; or if – not to be buried
> But quick and in mine arms
>
> (4.4.127–32)

Whereas the dramatic verse shows Perdita plunging between possibilities in the heat of a moment that intimates – just intimates – the mortal seriousness of a love that can join two people until death does them part, the sonnet's spirit dwells on an ambiguous place where love lives surrounded by the trophies of the dead. The sonnet does not imitate a delighted play with the powers of love and death but invites the reader to share the point of view of someone shaken by something he dares not approach too directly. In the play the writer has his eye upon the theatre; in the sonnet he follows a thought where it leads him. Shakespeare's sonnets present not scenes from the drama of love but the process of thinking feeling and feeling thinking. To this they owe their unique quality of intimacy.

It is this that adds point to the natural question: what

underlies these sonnets' dedication to a man? Shakespeare's sonnets are the only ones among the major sequences to be focused on a man. Is the special quality of these poems to be explained by a unique quality in the relationship they describe? Are the sonnets the record of an Elizabethan or Jacobean homosexual courtship? Fifty years ago the question was barely thinkable – though plainly it had been asked and, in fantasy terms, answered by Oscar Wilde in his long essay-story 'The Portrait of Mr W. H.'.

Half a century ago it would have been said that the relationship depicted in the sonnets was not a sexual one but reflected a cult of ideal friendship between men, such as we meet in Sir Philip Sidney's prose romance, *Arcadia*. Pyrocles and Musidorus are not lovers, but their friendship is of a high strain, higher than we find in, for example, the early Elizabethan play *Damon and Pythias* where the two young men strive as to which will be allowed to sacrifice his life that the other may live. Another analogy might have been with the friendship of Michel de Montaigne for Etienne de la Boetie recorded in his *Essays*.

This line of argument seems not to cut much ice now. All the relationships cited in the previous paragraph were relations of equals. But Shakespeare is emphatically not the equal of his young man either in rank, age or looks. It gives to the poet a humility that is more appropriate to the poetry of love than friendship. And in Shakespeare's sonnets, too, there is an element of the sexual to confuse matters. It is certainly possible to read such a poem as Sonnet 42 in terms of friendship without sexual connotation, but the poem does put love for a woman in parallel with love for a man, so that the very idea of that second love can be coloured by the sexuality of the first. This complicates the resonances of such a line as 'If I lose thee, my loss is my love's gain', which means both that the poet's loss of his young man is a gain for his mistress and that his love is somehow intensified by the pain which he suffers for his friend's sake. The sonnet ends in the safe haven of heterosexual romance:

> But here's the joy: my friend and I are one.
> Sweet flattery! Then she loves but me alone.

But this relative security is reached through a series of reflections that bring the friendship between the two men uncomfortably close to sexuality.

The relationship which appears in Shakespeare's sonnets is too complex, too human, to conform easily or happily to the model of ideal male friendship as we find it in *Arcadia* or Montaigne.

But there are difficulties too in describing it as homosexual. For a start the word 'homosexual' itself did not exist in Shakespeare's day and it is difficult, though not impossible, to practise what we have no words for. In *Homosexuality in Renaissance England* (1982) Alan Bray concluded that the horror expressed at homosexual practice was so intense as to make it just about impossible to acknowledge its existence. A sexual relationship between two men was in all important senses unthinkable. This did not prevent men from embracing each other or sleeping together but it did prevent the association of sexuality with these actions in public discourse. Doubtless then as now, people experienced feelings for each other of a homosexual kind, but a kind of self-censorship about these things seems most likely to have operated in Shakespeare's time. What this means is that such feelings may be reflected in the sonnets and of an intense kind, and yet not be recognized as such by the writer himself. The sonnets are indeed the realm of complex and obscure feeling, at least in this matter of sexuality.

What is true of the sonnets is also true of 'A Lover's Complaint'. The 'fickle maid full pale' laments her seduction by a young man distinguished in looks and status in much the same way as the young man of the sonnets. Her complaint has at its heart the winning speech of the young man himself:

> O most potential love: vow, bond, nor space
> In thee hath neither sting, knot, nor confine,
> For thou art all, and all things else are thine.

This sounds more like the praise of love than its repudiation as false. It is as though, assuming the voice of the young man, the complaining lover assumes his cause as well. No wonder she concludes that

> all that borrow'd motion, seeming ow'd,
> Would yet again betray the fore-betray'd,
> And new pervert a reconciled maid.

Because her words are echoed by the surrounding hills, the poet describes hers as a 'double voice'. It is double also in the sense of speaking with two tongues, both in accusation and in favour of the young man. It is even a duplicitous voice in that it enables her not to recognize the love which her words express within their intent to revile, and in this refusal of recognition 'A Lover's Complaint', with its elaborate pastoral disguise, its fiction of nuns and love-tokens, its conscientious poetic archaisms and anomalies, nevertheless shares something with the sonnets – a poetry of the most devastating yet unself-knowing honesty.

MARTIN DODSWORTH

NOTE ON THE TEXT

Shakespeare's sonnets and 'A Lover's Complaint' present few problems to the editor, rather more to the annotator.

As far as the text is concerned, I have gone back to the first edition of 1609 and amended it conservatively in line with the practice of other twentieth-century editors. I have paid special attention to the work of my predecessor in Everyman, M. R. Ridley, and to the editions of W. G. Ingram and Theodore Redpath (1964, revised 1978) and of John Kerrigan (1986).

The text has been prepared with the modern reader in mind, not merely in the standardization of spelling but especially in the way in which past tense and past participles ending in *ed* have been treated. A word such as *watched* may be pronounced as two syllables or one in Shakespeare's English, depending on the context. In this edition it is spelled *watch'd* as one syllable, *watched* as two, and this rule is observed strictly except for words like *replied*, *tied* and *dyed*, where *repli'd*, *ti'd* and *dy'd* would distract the reader by the oddity of their appearance. There the reader must use his or her own sense of rhythm as a guide, just as in the case of words like *heaven*, *trying*, *even*, *flattery* where often a syllable has to be swallowed in order to produce the effect Shakespeare intended. All readers should be encouraged to read these poems out loud and to listen to their harmony and rhythm.

As for annotation, my aim has been to offer the reader basic aid whilst allowing for the relative unfamiliarity of Elizabethan English to most twentieth-century readers. The reader should not feel inhibited by the presence of notes. Shakespeare's poems are not puzzles to which the solution must be found at the bottom of the page. When individual words or phrases pull you up short and leave you uncertain of meaning, the annotation is simply meant to give you a hand.

THE SONNETS

TO. THE. ONLIE. BEGETTER. OF.
THESE. INSVING. SONNETS.
M^R. W. H. ALL. HAPPINESSE.
AND. THAT. ETERNITIES.
PROMISED.

BY.

OVR. EVER-LIVING. POET.

WISHETH.

THE. WELL-WISHING.
ADVENTVRER. IN.
SETTING.
FORTH.

T.T

From fairest creatures we desire increase,
That thereby beauty's rose might never die,
But as the riper should by time decease,
His tender heir might bear his memory:
But thou, contracted to thine own bright eyes,
Feed'st thy light's flame with self-substantial fuel,
Making a famine where abundance lies,
Thyself thy foe, to thy sweet self too cruel.
Thou that art now the world's fresh ornament
And only herald to the gaudy spring
Within thine own bud buriest thy content,
And, tender churl, mak'st waste in niggarding.
  Pity the world, or else this glutton be,
  To eat the world's due, by the grave and thee.

---

5 *contracted*] betrothed   10 *gaudy*] bright (no detrimental sense)
12 *mak'st waste in niggarding*] are wasteful by being miserly (with yourself)
14 *the world's due, by the grave and thee*] your children, consumed by you in
your self-concern, and by death who consumes you

2

When forty winters shall besiege thy brow
And dig deep trenches in thy beauty's field,
Thy youth's proud livery, so gaz'd on now,
Will be a tatter'd weed of small worth held.
Then being ask'd where all thy beauty lies,
Where all the treasure of thy lusty days,
To say, within thine own deep-sunken eyes
Were an all-eating shame and thriftless praise.
How much more praise deserv'd thy beauty's use,
If thou couldst answer 'This fair child of mine
Shall sum my count and make my old excuse,'
Proving his beauty by succession thine.
    This were to be new made when thou art old,
    And see thy blood warm when thou feel'st it cold.

3 *proud livery*] uniform of which you are proud   4 *weed*] piece of clothing
8 *thriftless praise*] unprofitable form of praise   9 How much more would
putting your beauty to use deserve praise   11 *sum my count*] make up the
balance of my account; *make my old excuse*] make justification for me in my
old age

3

Look in thy glass, and tell the face thou viewest
Now is the time that face should form another,
Whose fresh repair if now thou not renewest,
Thou dost beguile the world, unbless some mother.
For where is she so fair whose unear'd womb
Disdains the tillage of thy husbandry?
Or who is he so fond, will be the tomb
Of his self-love to stop posterity?
Thou art thy mother's glass, and she in thee
Calls back the lovely April of her prime:
So thou through windows of thine age shalt see,
Despite of wrinkles, this thy golden time.
  But if thou live remember'd not to be,
  Die single, and thine image dies with thee.

1 *glass*] mirror 3 *repair*] condition 4 *beguile*] cheat; *unbless some mother*] frustrate someone of motherhood 5 *unear'd*] unploughed 6 *tillage of thy husbandry*] cultivation by you as husband, farmer 7 *fond*] foolish 9 *glass*] mirror 11 *windows of thine age*] your eyes in age 13 *remember'd not to be*] to be forgotten

4

Unthrifty loveliness, why dost thou spend
Upon thyself thy beauty's legacy?
Nature's bequest gives nothing, but doth lend,
And being frank, she lends to those are free.
Then, beauteous niggard, why dost thou abuse
The bounteous largess given thee to give?
Profitless usurer, why dost thou use
So great a sum of sums, yet canst not live?
For having traffic with thyself alone,
Thou of thyself thy sweet self dost deceive.
Then how, when nature calls thee to be gone,
What acceptable audit canst thou leave?
     Thy unus'd beauty must be tomb'd with thee,
     Which, used, lives th'executor to be.

1 *Unthrifty*] wasteful, unprofitable   4 *frank*] open, generous; *free*] generous materially and sexually   7 *use*] make use of, use up   8 *live*] live
life fully, perpetuate yourself   9 *having traffic with*] having to do with
12 *audit*] account of yourself   13 *unus'd*] put to no profit   14 *executor*]
person entrusted with carrying out the wishes of the deceased

5

Those hours that with gentle work did frame
The lovely gaze where every eye doth dwell
Will play the tyrants to the very same,
And that unfair which fairly doth excel:
For never-resting time leads summer on
To hideous winter, and confounds him there,
Sap check'd with frost, and lusty leaves quite gone,
Beauty o'er-snow'd, and bareness everywhere.
Then were not summer's distillation left,
A liquid prisoner pent in walls of glass,
Beauty's effect with beauty were bereft –
Nor it, nor no remembrance what it was.
    But flowers distill'd, though they with winter meet,
    Leese but their show; their substance still lives sweet.

4 *that unfair which fairly*] make that ugly which in its beauty   6 *confounds*] destroys   9 *summer's distillation*] summer's essence, its perfume   11 *were bereft*] would be taken away   12 Neither beauty nor memory of what beauty was would be left   14 *Leese*] lose

6

Then let not winter's ragged hand deface
In thee thy summer ere thou be distill'd:
Make sweet some vial, treasure thou some place
With beauty's treasure ere it be self-kill'd.
That use is not forbidden usury
Which happies those that pay the willing loan:
That's for thyself to breed another thee,
Or ten times happier, be it ten for one;
Ten times thyself were happier than thou art,
If ten of thine ten times refigur'd thee:
Then what could death do if thou shouldst depart,
Leaving thee living in posterity?
   Be not self-will'd, for thou art much too fair
   To be death's conquest and make worms thine heir.

1 *ragged*] coarse, dressed in tatters   3 *treasure*] make rich   5 *forbidden
usury*] usury (lending for interest) was legal but not universally approved, and
many moral distinctions were possible   6 *happies*] makes happy; *pay the
willing loan*] willingly pay interest on the loan   7 *That's for thyself to*] that
form of usury is when you   8 *be it ten for one*] if one of you creates ten
more of you (playing on the idea of interest rates)   10 *refigur'd thee*]
remade you (in the form of a hundred grandchildren – also playing on the idea
of figures in an account-book)

7

Lo, in the orient when the gracious light
Lifts up his burning head, each under eye
Doth homage to his new-appearing sight,
Serving with looks his sacred majesty,
And having climb'd the steep-up heavenly hill,
Resembling strong youth in his middle age,
Yet mortal looks adore his beauty still,
Attending on his golden pilgrimage;
But when from highmost pitch, with weary car,
Like feeble age he reeleth from the day,
The eyes, 'fore duteous, now converted are
From his low tract, and look another way.
  So thou, thyself outgoing in thy noon,
  Unlook'd on diest unless thou get a son.

1 *orient*] east; *light*] sun 2 *under*] inferior by being on the ground and/or in rank 5 *steep-up*] precipitous 7 *Yet mortal looks adore*] nevertheless the gaze of mortals reverences 9 *car*] chariot (of the sun-god) 11 *converted*] turned away 12 *tract*] path 13 *outgoing*] surpassing

8

Music to hear, why hear'st thou music sadly?
Sweets with sweets war not, joy delights in joy;
Why lov'st thou that which thou receiv'st not gladly,
Or else receiv'st with pleasure thine annoy?
If the true concord of well-tuned sounds,
By unions married, do offend thine ear,
They do but sweetly chide thee, who confounds
In singleness the parts that thou shouldst bear.
Mark how one string, sweet husband to another,
Strikes each in each by mutual ordering,
Resembling sire and child and happy mother,
Who, all in one, one pleasing note do sing;
    Whose speechless song, being many, seeming one,
    Sings this to thee: 'Thou single wilt prove none.'

1 *Music to hear*] You who are music to hear   5 *concord*] harmony   6 *By unions married*] brought together in satisfying matches   8 *singleness*] un-married state; *parts*] diverse musical lines, different roles (husband, father) to be played   10 *Strikes . . . ordering*] (Probably alludes to the double-strung lute in which two strings, tuned sympathetically, sound the same note)   14 *Thou single wilt prove none*] cf. the proverb 'One is no number'

9

Is it for fear to wet a widow's eye
That thou consum'st thyself in single life?
Ah! if thou issueless shalt hap to die,
The world will wail thee like a makeless wife.
The world will be thy widow, and still weep
That thou no form of thee hast left behind,
When every private widow well may keep
By children's eyes her husband's shape in mind.
Look, what an unthrift in the world doth spend
Shifts but his place, for still the world enjoys it;
But beauty's waste hath in the world an end,
And kept unus'd, the user so destroys it.
    No love toward others in that bosom sits
    That on himself such murd'rous shame commits.

1 *wet a widow's eye*] make a widow weep   3 *issueless*] childless   4 *wail*]
mourn for; *makeless*] without a mate   6 *form*] likeness   7 *private*]
separate   8 *By*] by means of   9 *unthrift*] prodigal   10 *his*] its
11 *beauty's waste*] beauty wasted like the prodigal's money

10

For shame, deny that thou bear'st love to any,
Who for thyself art so unprovident.
Grant, if thou wilt, thou art belov'd of many,
But that thou none lov'st is most evident;
For thou art so possess'd with murd'rous hate
That 'gainst thyself thou stick'st not to conspire,
Seeking that beauteous roof to ruinate
Which to repair should be thy chief desire.
O, change thy thought, that I may change my mind!
Shall hate be fairer lodg'd than gentle love?
Be as thy presence is, gracious and kind,
Or to thyself at least kind-hearted prove.
    Make thee another self, for love of me,
    That beauty still may live in thine or thee.

6   *stick'st not*] do not hesitate   7   *roof*] house, family   11   *presence*] appearance

11

As fast as thou shalt wane, so fast thou grow'st
In one of thine from that which thou departest,
And that fresh blood which youngly thou bestow'st
Thou mayst call thine when thou from youth convertest.
Herein lives wisdom, beauty, and increase;
Without this, folly, age, and cold decay.
If all were minded so, the times should cease,
And threescore year would make the world away.
Let those whom nature hath not made for store,
Harsh, featureless, and rude, barrenly perish.
Look whom she best endow'd she gave the more,
Which bounteous gift thou shouldst in bounty cherish.
     She carv'd thee for her seal, and meant thereby
     Thou shouldst print more, not let that copy die.

2 *one of thine*] a child of yours; *that which thou departest*] your youth   4 *con-vertest*] turn away   7 *so*] like you   8 *make the world away*] see the end of the world   9 *for store*] as stock to be drawn on   10 *barrenly*] without children   12 *in bounty*] with generosity   13 *seal*] an engraved stone with which to seal wax, a stamp of authority   14 *copy*] design

12

When I do count the clock that tells the time,
And see the brave day sunk in hideous night;
When I behold the violet past prime,
And sable curls all silver'd o'er with white;
When lofty trees I see barren of leaves,
Which erst from heat did canopy the herd,
And summer's green all girded up in sheaves
Borne on the bier with white and bristly beard:
Then of thy beauty do I question make,
That thou among the wastes of time must go,
Since sweets and beauties do themselves forsake,
And die as fast as they see others grow;
  And nothing 'gainst Time's scythe can make defence
  Save breed, to brave him when he takes thee hence.

6 *erst*] formerly   8 *bier*] barrow   9 *of thy beauty do I question make*] I ponder your beauty questioningly   10 *among the wastes of time*] where Time's waste things go   11 *themselves forsake*] change in their nature 14 *Save breed, to brave him*] except children, to defy Time

13

O that you were yourself; but, love, you are
No longer yours than you yourself here live:
Against this coming end you should prepare,
And your sweet semblance to some other give.
So should that beauty which you hold in lease
Find no determination; then you were
Yourself again after your self's decease,
When your sweet issue your sweet form should bear.
Who lets so fair a house fall to decay,
Which husbandry in honour might uphold
Against the stormy gusts of winter's day
And barren rage of death's eternal cold?
    O, none but unthrifts, dear my love, you know.
    You had a father; let your son say so.

3 *Against*] in expectation of   5 *in lease*] for a given period of time
6 *determination*] conclusion (legally a lease at its conclusion has 'determined')
10 *husbandry*] good housekeeping with a pun on 'being a husband')

14

Not from the stars do I my judgement pluck,
And yet methinks I have astronomy;
But not to tell of good or evil luck,
Of plagues, of dearths, or seasons' quality.
Nor can I fortune to brief minutes tell,
Pointing to each his thunder, rain, and wind,
Or say with princes if it shall go well
By oft predict that I in heaven find.
But from thine eyes my knowledge I derive,
And, constant stars, in them I read such art
As truth and beauty shall together thrive
If from thyself to store thou wouldst convert;
    Or else of thee this I prognosticate:
    Thy end is truth's and beauty's doom and date.

2 *astronomy*] astrology   6 *Pointing to each*] assigning to each minute 8 *By oft . . . find*] by frequent predictions based on what I find in the skies 10–11 *read such art/ As*] discover the knowledge that   12 *store*] breeding children; *convert*] turn   14 *date*] last day

15

When I consider every thing that grows
Holds in perfection but a little moment,
That this huge stage presenteth naught but shows
Whereon the stars in secret influence comment;
When I perceive that men as plants increase,
Cheered and check'd even by the selfsame sky,
Vaunt in their youthful sap, at height decrease,
And wear their brave state out of memory:
Then the conceit of this inconstant stay
Sets you most rich in youth before my sight,
Where wasteful Time debateth with Decay
To change your day of youth to sullied night;
     And all in war with Time for love of you,
     As he takes from you, I engraft you new.

---

4 *in secret influence comment*] exercise an inscrutable influence according to their judgment   6 *Cheered and check'd*] encouraged and restrained   7 *Vaunt*] exult   8 *wear . . . memory*] wear their finery until it is worn out and forgotten   9 *conceit*] thought   11 *debateth*] contests   13 *all in war*] utterly at war   14 *engraft you new*] give you new life (by writing about you)

16

But wherefore do not you a mightier way
Make war upon this bloody tyrant, Time,
And fortify yourself in your decay
With means more blessed than my barren rhyme?
Now stand you on the top of happy hours,
And many maiden gardens yet unset
With virtuous wish would bear your living flowers,
Much liker than your painted counterfeit.
So should the lines of life that life repair
Which this time's pencil or my pupil pen
Neither in inward worth nor outward fair
Can make you live yourself in eyes of men.
  To give away yourself keeps yourself still;
  And you must live, drawn by your own sweet skill.

1 *mightier*] more powerful (than through my verses about you)   3 *fortify*] strengthen   6 *unset*] unplanted   8 *liker*] more like you; *counterfeit*] portrait   9 *the lines of life*] the line which, by having children, the young man would continue   10 *this time's pencil*] the brush of today's artist 11 *fair*] beauty   13 *give away yourself*] i.e. in marriage or in your children

17

Who will believe my verse in time to come,
If it were fill'd with your most high deserts?
– Though yet, heaven knows, it is but as a tomb
Which hides your life, and shows not half your parts.
If I could write the beauty of your eyes
And in fresh numbers number all your graces,
The age to come would say 'This poet lies;
Such heavenly touches ne'er touch'd earthly faces.'
So should my papers, yellow'd with their age,
Be scorn'd, like old men of less truth than tongue,
And your true rights be term'd a poet's rage
And stretched metre of an antique song.
But were some child of yours alive that time,
You should live twice: in it, and in my rhyme.

6 *numbers*] verses   11 *your true rights*] your due in all truth; *a poet's rage*] the product of poetic hyperbole   12 *stretched metre*] exaggerated measure; *antique*] (pronounced 'antic') ancient

18

Shall I compare thee to a summer's day?
Thou art more lovely and more temperate.
Rough winds do shake the darling buds of May,
And summer's lease hath all too short a date;
Sometime too hot the eye of heaven shines,
And often is his gold complexion dimm'd,
And every fair from fair sometime declines,
By chance or nature's changing course untrimm'd;
But thy eternal summer shall not fade
Nor lose possession of that fair thou ow'st,
Nor shall death brag thou wander'st in his shade,
When in eternal lines to time thou grow'st.
    So long as men can breathe or eyes can see,
    So long lives this, and this gives life to thee.

---

4   *date*] time allotted to it   7   *fair from fair*] beautiful thing from beauty
8   *untrimm'd*] stripped of ornament   10   *fair thou ow'st*] beauty you own
12   *lines*] verse, and possibly lines of descent; *to time thou grow'st*] you reach
as far as time will go   14   *this*] this sonnet, and possibly the truth it conveys

19

Devouring Time, blunt thou the lion's paws,
And make the earth devour her own sweet brood;
Pluck the keen teeth from the fierce tiger's jaws,
And burn the long-liv'd phoenix in her blood;
Make glad and sorry seasons as thou fleet'st,
And do whate'er thou wilt, swift-footed Time,
To the wide world and all her fading sweets;
But I forbid thee one most heinous crime.
O, carve not with thy hours my love's fair brow,
Nor draw no lines there with thine antique pen.
Him in thy course untainted do allow
For beauty's pattern to succeeding men.
  Yet do thy worst, old Time; despite thy wrong,
  My love shall in my verse ever live young.

4   *phoenix*] bird supposed to be consumed periodically in flames and then to
revive. There was only one phoenix in the world   10   *antique*] (pronounced
'antic') ancient   11   *untainted*] untouched, unsullied

20

A woman's face with Nature's own hand painted
Hast thou, the master-mistress of my passion;
A woman's gentle heart, but not acquainted
With shifting change as is false women's fashion;
An eye more bright than theirs, less false in rolling,
Gilding the object whereupon it gazeth;
A man in hue, all hues in his controlling,
Which steals men's eyes and women's souls amazeth.
And for a woman wert thou first created,
Till Nature as she wrought thee fell a-doting,
And by addition me of thee defeated
By adding one thing to my purpose nothing.
    But since she prick'd thee out for women's pleasure,
    Mine be thy love, and thy love's use their treasure.

1   *with Nature's own hand painted*] i.e. naturally not cosmetically beautiful
5   *rolling*] passing from one to another   6   *Gilding*] adding lustre to
7   *A man in hue*] a man in appearance, a fine man; *all hues in his controlling*]
to whom all others are subject, or which may command every aspect of human
form (e.g. both male and female)   10   *fell a-doting*] became besotted
11   *addition*] adding something (a penis)   13   *prick'd*] marked (with a
quibble, as in 'thing' in the previous line)

21

So is it not with me as with that Muse
Stirr'd by a painted beauty to his verse,
Who heaven itself for ornament doth use,
And every fair with his fair doth rehearse,
Making a couplement of proud compare
With sun and moon, with earth and sea's rich gems,
With April's first-born flowers, and all things rare
That heaven's air in this huge rondure hems.
O let me, true in love, but truly write,
And then believe me, my love is as fair
As any mother's child, though not so bright
As those gold candles fix'd in heaven's air.
    Let them say more that like of hearsay well;
    I will not praise, that purpose not to sell.

1   *Muse*] poet   2   *Stirr'd*] who is inspired; *painted*] i.e. artificially derived
4   *fair with his fair*] beautiful thing with his beauty; *rehearse*] join together in
his words   5   *Making a couplement of proud compare*] linking the subject
of his praise in fine comparison   8   *rondure*] round of the world or universe
9   *but truly*] only with truth   13   *hearsay*] empty talk

22

My glass shall not persuade me I am old
So long as youth and thou are of one date;
But when in thee time's furrows I behold,
Then look I death my days should expiate.
For all that beauty that doth cover thee
Is but the seemly raiment of my heart,
Which in thy breast doth live, as thine in me;
How can I then be elder than thou art?
O therefore, love, be of thyself so wary
As I, not for myself, but for thee will,
Bearing thy heart, which I will keep so chary
As tender nurse her babe from faring ill.
    Presume not on thy heart when mine is slain:
    Thou gav'st me thine not to give back again.

---

1 *glass*] mirror   2 *of one date*] to be identified one with the other
4 *expiate*] end   6 *seemly*] handsome   11 *chary*] carefully

23

As an unperfect actor on the stage,
Who with his fear is put besides his part,
Or some fierce thing replete with too much rage,
Whose strength's abundance weakens his own heart,
So I, for fear of trust, forget to say
The perfect ceremony of love's rite,
And in mine own love's strength seem to decay,
O'er-charg'd with burden of mine own love's might.
O let my books be then the eloquence
And dumb presagers of my speaking breast,
Who plead for love, and look for recompense
More than that tongue that more hath more express'd.
    O, learn to read what silent love hath writ;
    To hear with eyes belongs to love's fine wit.

1 *unperfect*] ill-prepared 5 *for fear of trust*] because I lack trust (in myself or, possibly, you) 6 *rite*] ritual, but also right 7 *decay*] weaken, falter 9 *books*] writings (probably these poems) 10 *presagers*] heralds; *speaking*] (though silent) 12 *more hath more*] has more often or more finely, more copiously

24

Mine eye hath play'd the painter, and hath stell'd
Thy beauty's form in table of my heart.
My body is the frame wherein 'tis held,
And perspective it is best painter's art;
For through the painter must you see his skill
To find where your true image pictur'd lies,
Which in my bosom's shop is hanging still,
That hath his windows glazed with thine eyes.
Now see what good turns eyes for eyes have done:
Mine eyes have drawn thy shape, and thine for me
Are windows to my breast, wherethrough the sun
Delights to peep, to gaze therein on thee.
    Yet eyes this cunning want to grace their art:
    They draw but what they see, know not the heart.

1 *stell'd*] delineated   2 *in table*] on the ground   4 *perspective*] seen from the right point of view   5 *through the painter*] by looking through my eyes (which have *play'd the painter*)   7 *bosom's shop*] heart, where the *painter* keeps his stock   8 *his windows glazed with thine eyes*] my eyes *glazed* with yours (because your gaze is reflected in them)   13 *this cunning want*] lack this skill

25

Let those who are in favour with their stars
Of public honour and proud titles boast,
Whilst I, whom fortune of such triumph bars,
Unlook'd-for joy in that I honour most.
Great princes' favourites their fair leaves spread
But as the marigold at the sun's eye,
And in themselves their pride lies buried,
For at a frown they in their glory die.
The painful warrior famoused for might,
After a thousand victories once foil'd
Is from the book of honour razed quite,
And all the rest forgot for which he toil'd.
    Then happy I, that love and am belov'd
    Where I may not remove nor be remov'd.

4 *Unlook'd-for*] unregarded, and against expectation; *joy in that*] delight in the person, or in the fact that   6 *marigold*] flower which opens and shuts depending on the sun's intensity   9 *painful*] both causing and suffering pain; *famoused*] renowned   11 *razed*] erased   14 *remove*] change affection; *be remov'd*] (from favour)

26

Lord of my love, to whom in vassalage
Thy merit hath my duty strongly knit,
To thee I send this written ambassage
To witness duty, not to show my wit –
Duty so great which wit so poor as mine
May make seem bare in wanting words to show it,
But that I hope some good conceit of thine
In thy soul's thought, all naked, will bestow it;
Till whatsoever star that guides my moving
Points on me graciously with fair aspect,
And puts apparel on my tatter'd loving
To show me worthy of thy sweet respect.
     Then may I dare to boast how I do love thee;
     Till then, not show my head where thou mayst prove me.

1 *vassalage*] allegiance   3 *ambassage*] message   4 *wit*] skill   5 *wit*] intelligence   6 *wanting*] lacking   7 *good conceit*] kind opinion, good literary idea   8 *bestow it*] find a place for it (in all its nakedness)   10 *Points*] directs its rays; *aspect*] (accentuated on the second syllable)   14 *prove me*] put me to the test

27

Weary with toil I haste me to my bed,
The dear repose for limbs with travel tir'd;
But then begins a journey in my head
To work my mind when body's work's expir'd;
For then my thoughts, from far where I abide,
Intend a zealous pilgrimage to thee,
And keep my drooping eyelids open wide,
Looking on darkness which the blind do see:
Save that my soul's imaginary sight
Presents thy shadow to my sightless view,
Which like a jewel hung in ghastly night
Makes black night beauteous and her old face new.
    Lo, thus by day my limbs, by night my mind,
    For thee, and for myself, no quiet find.

2 *travel*] journeying, and work   4 *expir'd*] concluded at the end of day, and in sleep   6 *Intend*] go on   9 *imaginary*] imaginative, imaging 10 *shadow*] image; *sightless view*] unseeing vision

28

How can I then return in happy plight,
That am debarr'd the benefit of rest,
When day's oppression is not eas'd by night,
But day by night and night by day oppress'd,
And each, though enemies to either's reign,
Do in consent shake hands to torture me,
The one by toil, the other to complain
How far I toil, still farther off from thee?
I tell the day, to please him thou art bright,
And dost him grace when clouds do blot the heaven;
So flatter I the swart-complexion'd night,
When sparkling stars twire not, thou gild'st the even.
    But day doth daily draw my sorrows longer,
        And night doth nightly make grief's strength seem
            stronger.

6 *shake hands*] agree   7 *the other to complain*] i.e. night tortures me by
encouraging me to make complaint   11 *swart-complexion'd*] dark-
complexioned   12 *When*] i.e. to the effect that when; *twire*] peep; *gild'st
the even*] make bright the dark

29

When, in disgrace with Fortune and men's eyes,
I all alone beweep my outcast state,
And trouble deaf heaven with my bootless cries,
And look upon myself and curse my fate,
Wishing me like to one more rich in hope,
Featur'd like him, like him with friends possess'd,
Desiring this man's art and that man's scope,
With what I most enjoy contented least:
Yet in these thoughts myself almost despising,
Haply I think on thee, and then my state,
Like to the lark at break of day arising,
From sullen earth sings hymns at heaven's gate;
    For thy sweet love remember'd such wealth brings
    That then I scorn to change my state with kings.

1 *in disgrace*] out of favour   3 *bootless*] pointless   7 *art*] skill; *scope*] range   8 *most enjoy*] have most of, and take most pleasure in   10 *Haply*] by chance   12 *From sullen earth*] Leaving dark and heavy earth (my discontent)

30

When to the sessions of sweet silent thought
I summon up remembrance of things past,
I sigh the lack of many a thing I sought,
And with old woes new wail my dear time's waste.
Then can I drown an eye, unus'd to flow,
For precious friends hid in death's dateless night,
And weep afresh love's long since cancell'd woe,
And moan th'expense of many a vanish'd sight.
Then can I grieve at grievances foregone,
And heavily from woe to woe tell o'er
The sad account of fore-bemoaned moan,
Which I new pay as if not paid before.
   But if the while I think on thee, dear friend,
   All losses are restor'd, and sorrows end.

---

1 *sessions*] court sittings (cf. 'summon up' in next line) 3 *sigh*] sigh for
4 *new wail my dear time's waste*] lament once more how my precious time has
been wasted, or laid waste (by the death of friends) 5 *flow*] i.e. in tears
6 *dateless*] unending 7 *cancell'd*] paid off 8 *expense of many a
vanish'd sight*] passing of many a thing seen, expenditure of many a sigh in the
past 9 *foregone*] that are past or given over 10 *heavily*] sadly
11 *fore-bemoaned moan*] laments already once or more lamented

31

Thy bosom is endeared with all hearts
Which I by lacking have supposed dead;
And there reigns love, and all love's loving parts,
And all those friends which I thought buried.
How many a holy and obsequious tear
Hath dear religious love stol'n from mine eye
As interest of the dead, which now appear
But things remov'd that hidden in thee lie!
Thou art the grave where buried love doth live,
Hung with the trophies of my lovers gone,
Who all their parts of me to thee did give:
That due of many now is thine alone.
　　Their images I loved I view in thee,
　　And thou, all they, hast all the all of me.

1 *endeared with*] made more precious by　2 *lacking*] not having (because they are dead (cf. the previous sonnet))　5 *obsequious*] funereal　7 *interest of*] what is due to　9 *buried*] (two syllables)　11 *parts of me*] shares in me　12 *That due of many*] what was owed to many (my love)　13 *Their images I loved*] the images of those whom I loved

32

If thou survive my well-contented day
When that churl Death my bones with dust shall cover,
And shalt by fortune once more re-survey
These poor rude lines of thy deceased lover,
Compare them with the bett'ring of the time,
And though they be outstripp'd by every pen,
Reserve them for my love, not for their rhyme,
Exceeded by the height of happier men.
O, then vouchsafe me but this loving thought:
'Had my friend's Muse grown with this growing age,
A dearer birth than this his love had brought
To march in ranks of better equipage;
    But since he died, and poets better prove,
    Theirs for their style I'll read, his for his love.'

---

1   *well-contented day*] the day of my death at which I shall not repine   5   *Compare them with the bett'ring of the time*] Read them alongside the improved style of that later time   7   *Reserve*] preserve   8   *Exceeded by the height of happier men*] outdone by the achievement of more fortunate writers   10   *Muse grown with this growing age*] art developed as this age progressed   11–12   My love for him would have produced a more precious creation to find its place among more elegant works

33

Full many a glorious morning have I seen
Flatter the mountain tops with sovereign eye,
Kissing with golden face the meadows green,
⸺lding pale streams with heavenly alchemy,
Anon permit the basest clouds to ride
With ugly rack on his celestial face,
And from the forlorn world his visage hide,
Stealing unseen to west with this disgrace.
Even so my sun one early morn did shine
With all triumphant splendour on my brow,
But out, alack, he was but one hour mine;
The region cloud hath mask'd him from me now.
     Yet him for this my love no whit disdaineth;
     Suns of the world may stain when heaven's sun staineth.

2 *Flatter*] dignify beyond their due; *sovereign eye*] royal countenance (of the sun)   4 *Gilding*] turning to gold   6 *rack*] driving clouds   7 *forlorn*] (accented on the first syllable)   12 *region*] belonging to the upper air   13 *no whit*] not at all   14 *stain*] lose lustre

34

Why didst thou promise such a beauteous day
And make me travel forth without my cloak,
To let base clouds o'ertake me in my way,
Hiding thy brav'ry in their rotten smoke?
'Tis not enough that through the cloud thou break
To dry the rain on my storm-beaten face,
For no man well of such a salve can speak
That heals the wound and cures not the disgrace:
Nor can thy shame give physic to my grief;
Though thou repent, yet I have still the loss.
Th' offender's sorrow lends but weak relief
To him that bears the strong offence's cross.
    Ah, but those tears are pearl which thy love sheds,
    And they are rich, and ransom all ill deeds.

3 *base*] dark   4 *brav'ry*] finery; *rotten smoke*] unwholesome breath
7 *salve*] palliative or remedy   9 *thy shame give physic to*] your being
ashamed be a medicine for   12 *bears the . . . cross*] suffers the pain
14 *ransom*] make up for

35

No more be griev'd at that which thou hast done:
Roses have thorns, and silver fountains mud,
Clouds and eclipses stain both moon and sun,
And loathsome canker lives in sweetest bud.
All men make faults, and even I in this,
Authorizing thy trespass with compare,
Myself corrupting, salving thy amiss,
Excusing thy sins more than thy sins are;
For to thy sensual fault I bring in sense –
Thy adverse party is thy advocate –
And 'gainst myself a lawful plea commence,
Such civil war is in my love and hate,
    That I an accessory needs must be
    To that sweet thief which sourly robs from me.

3 *stain*] darken   4 *canker*] destructive worm, grub, etc.   6 Justifying your wrongdoing by comparisons (*authorizing* is accented on the second syllable)   7 *salving*] making good; *amiss*] offence   8 Producing excuses for more (or worse) sins than those you have actually committed   9 *bring in sense*] bring intellect to help   10 The person opposing you speaks in your behalf   11 *commence*] the proper term for beginning an action in law   14 *sourly*] with bitter effect

36

Let me confess that we two must be twain,
Although our undivided loves are one;
So shall those blots that do with me remain,
Without thy help by me be borne alone.
In our two loves there is but one respect,
Though in our lives a separable spite,
Which, though it alter not love's sole effect,
Yet doth it steal sweet hours from love's delight.
I may not evermore acknowledge thee,
Lest my bewailed guilt should do thee shame,
Nor thou with public kindness honour me
Unless thou take that honour from thy name.
    But do not so. I love thee in such sort
    As, thou being mine, mine is thy good report.

1 *be twain*] be parted, be separated one from another   3 *those blots*] defects inherent in me or acquired as a result of your conduct (cf. preceding sonnets)   5 *one respect*] one thing that matters   6 *separable spite*] pain of separation   9 *not evermore*] nevermore   10 *bewailed*] lamented 12 Without diminishing the honour due to your rank (*name* is both personal and family reputation)   13-14] (These lines also conclude Sonnet 96) 14 *report*] reputation

37

As a decrepit father takes delight
To see his active child do deeds of youth,
So I, made lame by fortune's dearest spite,
Take all my comfort of thy worth and truth;
For whether beauty, birth, or wealth, or wit,
Or any of these all, or all, or more,
Entitled in thy parts do crowned sit,
I make my love engrafted to this store:
So then I am not lame, poor, nor despis'd,
Whilst that this shadow doth such substance give
That I in thy abundance am suffic'd
And by a part of all thy glory live.
  Look what is best, that best I wish in thee:
  This wish I have; then ten times happy me.

---

3 *dearest*] most grievous   4 *of*] from   7 Sit like a king by right among your qualities   8 I graft my love to this stock of plenty   10 *this shadow*] your image, your reflected glory

38

How can my Muse want subject to invent
While thou dost breathe, that pour'st into my verse
Thine own sweet argument, too excellent
For every vulgar paper to rehearse?
O, give thyself the thanks, if aught in me
Worthy perusal stand against thy sight;
For who's so dumb that cannot write to thee,
When thou thyself dost give invention light?
Be thou the tenth Muse, ten times more in worth
Than those old nine which rhymers invocate,
And he that calls on thee, let him bring forth
Eternal numbers to outlive long date.
　　　If my slight Muse do please these curious days,
　　　The pain be mine, but thine shall be the praise.

1 *subject to invent*] subject-matter   3 *Thine own sweet argument*] pleasing
subject-matter of your own, yourself as that subject-matter   4 *vulgar paper*]
commonplace writing   6 *stand against*] meet   8 *give invention light*]
light the way for creation   9-10 (In classical mythology nine Muses
presided over all the arts)   12 *Eternal numbers*] everlasting verses; *long
date*] far-off time   13 *curious*] fastidious, demanding

39

O, how thy worth with manners may I sing,
When thou art all the better part of me?
What can mine own praise to mine own self bring –
And what is 't but mine own when I praise thee?
Even for this let us divided live,
And our dear love lose name of single one,
That by this separation I may give
That due to thee which thou deserv'st alone.
O Absence, what a torment wouldst thou prove
Were it not thy sour leisure gave sweet leave
To entertain the time with thoughts of love,
Which time and thoughts so sweetly dost deceive,
  And that thou teachest how to make one twain
  By praising him here, who doth hence remain!

1 *with manners*] decently, without praising myself 6 *name of single one*] reputation of uniqueness, of undividedness 12 *so sweetly dost deceive*] you beguile with great sweetness 13 *one twain*] one person two 14 By praising him as a present reality who is at the same time absent

40

Take all my loves, my love, yea, take them all:
What hast thou then more than thou hadst before?
No love, my love, that thou mayst true love call;
All mine was thine before thou hadst this more.
Then if for my love thou my love receivest,
I cannot blame thee for my love thou usest;
But yet be blam'd if thou thyself deceivest
By wilful taste of what thyself refusest.
I do forgive thy robb'ry, gentle thief,
Although thou steal thee all my poverty;
And yet, love knows it is a greater grief
To bear love's wrong than hate's known injury.
    Lascivious grace, in whom all ill well shows,
    Kill me with spites; yet we must not be foes.

1 *my loves*] the people I love or who love me, and the love I bear them or they bear me   3 (You had my *true love* before you took my other loves from me)   5 If out of affection for me you entertain the person I love (the lady of Sonnets 127-52?)   6 *for my love thou usest*] because you take advantage of my love, and the person I love   8 *wilful taste*] perverse sampling; *thyself*] i.e. your better self   10 *all my poverty*] all that I have in my poverty 13 *Lascivious grace*] wanton beauty (the phrase implies a mixture of admiration and impatient disapproval)   14 *spites*] injuries

41

Those pretty wrongs that liberty commits,
When I am sometime absent from thy heart,
Thy beauty and thy years full well befits,
For still temptation follows where thou art.
Gentle thou art, and therefore to be won,
Beauteous thou art, therefore to be assail'd;
And when a woman woos, what woman's son
Will sourly leave her till she have prevail'd?
Ay me! but yet thou mightst my seat forbear,
And chide thy beauty and thy straying youth,
Who lead thee in their riot even there
Where thou art forc'd to break a two-fold troth:
  Hers, by thy beauty tempting her to thee,
  Thine, by thy beauty being false to me.

1 *pretty*] delightful, trivial (with some irony); *liberty*] freedom which may
or may not be licentious 3 *befits*] singular verb for plural subject (*wrongs*)
4 *still*] continually 5 *Gentle*] without coarseness, of good birth 9 *my
seat forbear*] decline to take my place 11 *riot*] prodigal conduct

42

That thou hast her, it is not all my grief,
And yet it may be said I lov'd her dearly;
That she hath thee is of my wailing chief,
A loss in love that touches me more nearly.
Loving offenders, thus I will excuse ye:
Thou dost love her because thou know'st I love her,
And for my sake even so doth she abuse me,
Suff'ring my friend for my sake to approve her.
If I lose thee, my loss is my love's gain,
And losing her, my friend hath found that loss:
Both find each other, and I lose both twain,
And both for my sake lay on me this cross.
    But here's the joy: my friend and I are one.
    Sweet flattery! Then she loves but me alone.

3 *of my wailing chief*] the main cause of my grief   5 *Loving offenders*] you who offend me and love each other, who offend me because you love each other   7 *abuse*] deceive   8 *approve*] put to the test sexually 10 *losing her*] if I lose her   11 *and*] if (probably)   12 *cross*] burden

43

When most I wink, then do mine eyes best see,
For all the day they view things unrespected;
But when I sleep, in dreams they look on thee,
And, darkly bright, are bright in dark directed.
Then thou, whose shadow shadows doth make bright,
How would thy shadow's form form happy show
To the clear day with thy much clearer light,
When to unseeing eyes thy shade shines so!
How would, I say, mine eyes be blessed made
By looking on thee in the living day,
When in dead night thy fair imperfect shade
Through heavy sleep on sightless eyes doth stay!
    All days are nights to see till I see thee,
    And nights bright days when dreams do show thee me.

2 *unrespected*] not regarded   4 And, blindly seeing, are by their illumination in the dark given direction and purpose   5 *shadow shadows doth make bright*] image brings light to darkness   6 *thy shadow's form*] the substance underlying your image   7 *clear*] bright   8 *unseeing*] i.e. closed in sleep   11 *imperfect*] because only an image

44

If the dull substance of my flesh were thought,
Injurious distance should not stop my way;
For then, despite of space, I would be brought
From limits far remote where thou dost stay.
No matter then although my foot did stand
Upon the farthest earth remov'd from thee;
For nimble thought can jump both sea and land
As soon as think the place where he would be.
But ah, thought kills me that I am not thought,
To leap large lengths of miles when thou art gone,
But that, so much of earth and water wrought,
I must attend time's leisure with my moan,
    Receiving naught by elements so slow
    But heavy tears, badges of either's woe.

---

1 *dull*] heavy   2 *stop*] hinder   4 *where*] to where   11 *so much of earth and water wrought*] being myself made up of so much earth and water (according to the division of matter into four elements, earth, air, fire, water)   12 *attend time's leisure*] wait until time is able to favour me   13 *elements so slow*] i.e. earth and water   14 *heavy*] sad; *badges of either's woe*] marks of the sorrowful nature of either element (both relatively slow and heavy)

45

The other two, slight air and purging fire,
Are both with thee, wherever I abide;
The first my thought, the other my desire,
These present-absent with swift motion slide.
For when these quicker elements are gone
In tender embassy of love to thee,
My life, being made of four, with two alone
Sinks down to death, oppress'd with melancholy,
Until life's composition be recur'd
By those swift messengers return'd from thee,
Who even but now come back again, assur'd
Of thy fair health, recounting it to me.
    This told, I joy; but then no longer glad,
    I send them back again and straight grow sad.

---

1 *The other two*] i.e. elements; *slight*] thin; *purging*] purifying   4 *slide*]
(being here one moment and gone the next)   5 *quicker*] speedier, and more
instinct with life   6 *embassy*] mission   8 *melancholy*] despondency,
and the black bile, associated with *earth*, supposed to generate it   9 *life's
composition be recur'd*] the balance of elements making up life is restored

46

Mine eye and heart are at a mortal war
How to divide the conquest of thy sight,
Mine eye, my heart thy picture's sight would bar,
My heart, mine eye the freedom of that right.
My heart doth plead that thou in him dost lie,
A closet never pierc'd with crystal eyes,
But the defendant doth that plea deny,
And says in him thy fair appearance lies.
To 'cide this title is empanelled
A quest of thoughts, all tenants to the heart,
And by their verdict is determined
The clear eye's moiety and the dear heart's part,
    As thus: mine eye's due is thy outward part,
    And my heart's right thy inward love of heart.

2 *conquest*] spoils, property acquired by means other than inheritance
3–4 My eyes would deny sight of your picture to my heart, my heart would
deny my eyes the freedom to exercise their right of gazing at it   6 *crystal
eyes*] eyes clear as crystal (possibly ironic use of cliché)   9–10 To settle the
question of rightful ownership a jury of thoughts, all owing tribute to the heart,
has been brought together   12 *moiety*] share

47

Betwixt mine eye and heart a league is took,
And each doth good turns now unto the other.
When that mine eye is famish'd for a look,
Or heart in love with sighs himself doth smother,
With my love's picture then my eye doth feast,
And to the painted banquet bids my heart;
Another time mine eye is my heart's guest
And in his thoughts of love doth share a part.
So either by thy picture or my love,
Thyself away are present still with me;
For thou not farther than my thoughts canst move,
And I am still with them, and they with thee;
    Or if they sleep, thy picture in my sight
    Awakes my heart to heart's and eye's delight.

1 *a league is took*] an agreement has been reached   6 *painted banquet*]
(The heart feeds on *my love's picture*)   12 *still*] continually

48

How careful was I when I took my way
Each trifle under truest bars to thrust,
That to my use it might unused stay
From hands of falsehood, in sure wards of trust!
But thou, to whom my jewels trifles are,
Most worthy comfort, now my greatest grief,
Thou best of dearest and mine only care,
Art left the prey of every vulgar thief.
Thee have I not lock'd up in any chest
Save where thou art not, though I feel thou art –
Within the gentle closure of my breast,
From whence at pleasure thou mayst come and part;
    And even thence thou wilt be stol'n, I fear,
    For truth proves thievish for a prize so dear.

1 *took my way*] left on my journey   3 *to my use*] reserved for my use
3–4 *unused stay/ From hands of falsehood*] keep out of the hands of dis-
honest thieves   4 *wards*] guarded places   11 *gentle*] (because loving)
14 *truth*] honesty

49

Against that time, if ever that time come,
When I shall see thee frown on my defects,
Whenas thy love hath cast his utmost sum,
Call'd to that audit by advis'd respects;
Against that time when thou shalt strangely pass,
And scarcely greet me with that sun, thine eye,
When love, converted from the thing it was,
Shall reasons find of settled gravity;
Against that time do I ensconce me here
Within the knowledge of mine own desert,
And this my hand against myself uprear
To guard the lawful reasons on thy part.
        To leave poor me thou hast the strength of laws,
        Since why to love I can allege no cause.

1 *Against*] in preparation for   2 *defects*] (accent on the second syllable)
3 *cast his utmost sum*] made his final reckoning   4 *advis'd respects*] well-
weighed considerations   5 *strangely*] like a stranger   8 *of*] for
behaving with   9 *ensconce me*] fortify myself   10 *desert*] deserving

50

How heavy do I journey on the way,
When what I seek, my weary travel's end,
Doth teach that ease and that repose to say
'Thus far the miles are measur'd from thy friend.'
The beast that bears me, tired with my woe,
Plods dully on to bear that weight in me,
As if by some instinct the wretch did know
His rider lov'd not speed being made from thee.
The bloody spur cannot provoke him on
That sometimes anger thrusts into his hide,
Which heavily he answers with a groan
More sharp to me than spurring to his side;
    For that same groan doth put this in my mind:
    My grief lies onward and my joy behind.

1   *heavy*] sadly   8   *being made*] when it is made   11   *heavily*] sadly

51

Thus can my love excuse the slow offence
Of my dull bearer when from thee I speed:
From where thou art why should I haste me thence?
Till I return, of posting is no need.
O what excuse will my poor beast then find,
When swift extremity can seem but slow?
Then should I spur, though mounted on the wind;
In winged speed no motion shall I know.
Then can no horse with my desire keep pace;
Therefore desire, of perfect'st love being made,
Shall rein no dull flesh in his fiery race;
But love, for love, thus shall excuse my jade:
    Since from thee going he went wilful-slow,
    Towards thee I'll run and give him leave to go.

1 *my love*] (for you); *slow offence*] offence of going slowly   2 *dull bearer*]
horse   4 *posting*] riding fast   6 *swift extremity*] extreme speed
8 I shall not know I am moving even when I go with the speed of wings
11 *rein*] i.e. ride (emended from *neigh* (*naigh*) in the 1609 edition)   12 *for
love*] for its own sake   14 *go*] walk

52

So am I as the rich, whose blessed key
Can bring him to his sweet up-locked treasure,
The which he will not ev'ry hour survey,
For blunting the fine point of seldom pleasure.
Therefore are feasts so solemn and so rare,
Since, seldom coming, in the long year set,
Like stones of worth they thinly placed are,
Or captain jewels in the carcanet.
So is the time that keeps you as my chest,
Or as the wardrobe which the robe doth hide,
To make some special instant special blest
By new unfolding his imprison'd pride.
    Blessed are you whose worthiness gives scope,
    Being had, to triumph, being lack'd, to hope.

1 *rich*] rich man   4 *For blunting*] in case he should blunt; *seldom*] infrequent   8 *captain*] chief; *carcanet*] collar, necklace   12 *his*] its, the time's, the wardrobe's

53

What is your substance, whereof are you made,
That millions of strange shadows on you tend?
Since everyone hath, every one, one shade,
And you, but one, can every shadow lend.
Describe Adonis, and the counterfeit
Is poorly imitated after you;
On Helen's cheek all art of beauty set,
And you in Grecian tires are painted new.
Speak of the spring and foison of the year:
The one doth shadow of your beauty show,
The other as your bounty doth appear;
And you in every blessed shape we know.
    In all external grace you have some part,
    But you like none, none you, for constant heart.

2 *strange shadows*] likenesses of other people; *tend*] wait like servants or court followers   4 And in you, though you are only one person, every attribute of others can be found   5 *counterfeit*] description, inauthentic in comparison with you   8 *tires*] dress   9 *foison*] harvest

54

O, how much more doth beauty beauteous seem
By that sweet ornament which truth doth give!
The rose looks fair, but fairer we it deem
For that sweet odour which doth in it live.
The canker blooms have full as deep a dye
As the perfum'd tincture of the roses –
Hang on such thorns, and play as wantonly
When summer's breath their masked buds discloses;
But for their virtue only is their show
They live unwoo'd and unrespected fade –
Die to themselves. Sweet roses do not so;
Of their sweet deaths are sweetest odours made:
    And so of you, beauteous and lovely youth,
    When that shall vade, by verse distils your truth.

2 *truth*] integrity, constancy   5 *canker blooms*] dog roses, which have no perfume; *deep a dye*] rich a colour   6 *tincture*] colouring   7 *such*] similar; *play*] wave; *wantonly*] freely   8 *masked*] concealed (in the bud, which opens to the summer breeze)   9 But because their only goodness is in their appearance   10 *unrespected*] unregarded   11 *to themselves*] unregarded   12 (Perfume is made from roses)   14 When your beauty goes, or fades, your truth will distil into its essence by means of my verse

55

Not marble nor the gilded monuments
Of princes shall outlive this powerful rhyme,
But you shall shine more bright in these contents
Than unswept stone besmear'd with sluttish time.
When wasteful war shall statues overturn
And broils root out the work of masonry,
Nor Mars his sword nor war's quick fire shall burn
The living record of your memory.
'Gainst death and all oblivious enmity
Shall you pace forth; your praise shall still find room
Even in the eyes of all posterity
That wear this world out to the ending doom.
    So, till the judgement that yourself arise,
    You live in this, and dwell in lovers' eyes.

3 *these contents*] (stressed on the second syllable) what is contained in this *rhyme*   4 *stone*] funerary monument, or memorial stone set in a church floor; *with sluttish time*] in the course of, as a result of, time's slovenly passage 6 *broils*] battles, skirmishes   7 *Mars his sword*] the sword of Mars, Roman god of war; *quick*] vigorous, vital   9 *oblivious enmity*] forgetfulness hostile to your memory   12 That survive with this world to the doomsday that ends it   13 *judgement that yourself*] Day of Judgement when you

56

Sweet love, renew thy force; be it not said
Thy edge should blunter be than appetite,
Which but today by feeding is allay'd,
Tomorrow sharpen'd in his former might.
So, love, be thou; although today thou fill
Thy hungry eyes even till they wink with fullness,
Tomorrow see again, and do not kill
The spirit of love with a perpetual dullness.
Let this sad interim like the ocean be
Which parts the shore, where two contracted new
Come daily to the banks, that when they see
Return of love, more bless'd may be the view.
  Or call it winter, which, being full of care,
  Makes summer's welcome thrice more wish'd, more rare.

1 *love*] (the emotion) 2 *should blunter be*] is blunter; *appetite*] hunger, lust 6 *wink with fullness*] drop with being sated 9 *interim*] (two syllables: *Intrim* in 1609) temporary state of affairs 10 *contracted new*] newly contracted lovers 14 *wish'd*] wished for

57

Being your slave, what should I do but tend
Upon the hours and times of your desire?
I have no precious time at all to spend,
Nor services to do, till you require.
Nor dare I chide the world-without-end hour
Whilst I, my sovereign, watch the clock for you,
Nor think the bitterness of absence sour
When you have bid your servant once adieu;
Nor dare I question with my jealous thought
Where you may be, or your affairs suppose,
But, like a sad slave, stay and think of naught
Save, where you are, how happy you make those.
　　So true a fool is love that in your will,
　　Though you do anything, he thinks no ill.

1 *tend*] wait　　2 *of your desire*] when you want something (of me)
4 *require*] command, ask　　5 *world-without-end hour*] hour which seems to
have no end　　9 *jealous*] which is or which might be mistrustful　　10 *your
affairs suppose*] guess at the business that occupies you　　12 Except how
happy you make the people who are with you　　13 *will*] desire (capable of a
bad sense), also possibly Will (Shakespeare)

58

That god forbid, that made me first your slave,
I should in thought control your times of pleasure,
Or at your hand th'account of hours to crave,
Being your vassal bound to stay your leisure.
O, let me suffer, being at your beck,
Th'imprison'd absence of your liberty,
And patience, tame to sufferance, bide each check,
Without accusing you of injury.
Be where you list, your charter is so strong
That you yourself may privilege your time
To what you will; to you it doth belong
Yourself to pardon of self-doing crime.
    I am to wait, though waiting so be hell,
    Not blame your pleasure, be it ill or well.

1 *That god*] i.e. Love   2 *control*] call to account   4 *stay*] await
6 *imprison'd*] like a prison for me; *of your liberty*] created by your freedom
(with a hint of a bad sense – 'excessive freedom')   7 *tame to sufferance*]
meekly putting up with what has to be endured; *bide each check*] put up with
every snub   9 *charter*] document giving right to act as judge and to grant
rights to others   10 *privilege*] authorize   12 *of self-doing crime*] for a
crime you have yourself committed   13 *I am*] I am expected   14 *be it
ill or well*] whether what pleases you (possibly a sexual meaning here), or my
blaming it, is a good or bad thing

59

If there be nothing new, but that which is
Hath been before, how are our brains beguil'd,
Which, labouring for invention, bear amiss
The second burden of a former child!
O, that record could with a backward look,
Even of five hundred courses of the sun,
Show me your image in some antique book
Since mind at first in character was done,
That I might see what the old world could say
To this composed wonder of your frame;
Whether we are mended or whe'er better they,
Or whether revolution be the same.
    O sure I am, the wits of former days
    To subjects worse have given admiring praise.

2 *beguil'd*] misled   3–4 Which, labouring to find a theme or topic, mis-
takenly give birth to a child that has been born once already, i.e. which strive
for originality and are bound not to find it   5 *record*] (stressed on the second
syllable) memory, history   6 *courses of the sun*] years   7 *antique*]
(pronounced 'antic') old   8 Since thoughts were first set down in writing
10 *composed wonder of your frame*] harmonious miracle of your form
11 *mended*] improved   12 *revolution be the same*] cycles of time produce
no change   13 *wits*] men of gift

60

Like as the waves make towards the pebbled shore,
So do our minutes hasten to their end;
Each changing place with that which goes before,
In sequent toil all forwards do contend.
Nativity, once in the main of light,
Crawls to maturity, wherewith being crown'd
Crooked eclipses 'gainst his glory fight,
And Time that gave doth now his gift confound.
Time doth transfix the flourish set on youth
And delves the parallels in beauty's brow,
Feeds on the rarities of nature's truth,
And nothing stands but for his scythe to mow.
  And yet to times in hope my verse shall stand,
  Praising thy worth despite his cruel hand.

4 *In sequent toil*] labouring one after another; *contend*] strive 5 *Nativity*]
the new-born child; *main*] ocean (of light – the world) 7 *Crooked*] malignant
(the image is astrological) 8 *confound*] destroy 9 *transfix*] impale, as
on a weapon; *flourish*] embellishment, sign of health 10 *delves the*
parallels] digs the lines 11 *rarities of nature's truth*] finest things of nature's
perfection 13 *times in hope*] times only dreamt of as yet

61

Is it thy will thy image should keep open
My heavy eyelids to the weary night?
Dost thou desire my slumbers should be broken,
While shadows like to thee do mock my sight?
Is it thy spirit that thou send'st from thee
So far from home into my deeds to pry,
To find out shames and idle hours in me,
The scope and tenor of thy jealousy?
O, no, thy love, though much, is not so great;
It is my love that keeps mine eye awake,
Mine own true love that doth my rest defeat,
To play the watchman ever for thy sake.
　　For thee watch I, whilst thou dost wake elsewhere,
　　From me far off, with others all too near.

2 *weary night*] night in which (of which?) men are weary　　8 *scope and tenor*] focus and chief concern (probably applied to *shames and idle hours*) 12 *ever*] continually　13 *watch*] look out anxiously, and stay awake

62

Sin of self-love possesseth all mine eye,
And all my soul, and all my every part;
And for this sin there is no remedy,
It is so grounded inward in my heart.
Methinks no face so gracious is as mine,
No shape so true, no truth of such account;
And for myself mine own worth do define
As I all other in all worths surmount.
But when my glass shows me myself indeed,
Beated and chopp'd with tann'd antiquity,
Mine own self-love quite contrary I read –
Self so self-loving were iniquity.
    'Tis thee, my self, that for myself I praise,
    Painting my age with beauty of thy days.

4 *inward*] i.e. deeply   6 *truth*] constancy   8 *As*] as if; *other*] others
9 *glass*] mirror; *indeed*] as I really am   10 My skin tanned by age, wind-
beaten and cracked   11 *quite contrary I read*] I interpret quite differently
12 It would be wicked for one to love oneself in such a way   13 *for
myself*] in my place   14 Making my aged self beautiful with the attributes
of your youth

63

Against my love shall be as I am now,
With Time's injurious hand crush'd and o'erworn;
When hours have drain'd his blood and fill'd his brow
With lines and wrinkles; when his youthful morn
Hath travell'd on to age's steepy night,
And all those beauties whereof now he's king
Are vanishing, or vanish'd out of sight,
Stealing away the treasure of his spring:
For such a time do I now fortify
Against confounding age's cruel knife,
That he shall never cut from memory
My sweet love's beauty, though my lover's life.
　　His beauty shall in these black lines be seen,
　　And they shall live, and he in them still green.

1 *Against*] in preparation for the time when   2 *o'erworn*] worn out
5 *steepy*] fast declining   9 *fortify*] build defences   10 *confounding*]
destructive   11–13 (The young man's life will not survive, but his beauty
will, preserved in these verses)   14 *still green*] for ever flourishing

64

When I have seen by Time's fell hand defac'd
The rich proud cost of outworn buried age;
When sometime-lofty towers I see down raz'd,
And brass eternal slave to mortal rage;
When I have seen the hungry ocean gain
Advantage on the kingdom of the shore,
And the firm soil win of the wat'ry main,
Increasing store with loss and loss with store;
When I have seen such interchange of state,
Or state itself confounded to decay,
Ruin hath taught me thus to ruminate,
That Time will come and take my love away.
     This thought is as a death, which cannot choose
     But weep to have that which it fears to lose.

1 *fell*] cruel   2 *cost*] things gained at high cost; *outworn*] worn out, old-fashioned; *buried*] (two syllables) i.e. in the past   4 *brass eternal*] everlasting brass; *mortal rage*] death's fury   7 *main*] ocean   8 Each gaining as it loses and losing as it gains   9 *interchange of state*] exchange of condition 10 *state*] i.e. prosperous state

65

Since brass, nor stone, nor earth, nor boundless sea,
But sad mortality o'ersways their power,
How with this rage shall beauty hold a plea,
Whose action is no stronger than a flower?
O, how shall summer's honey breath hold out
Against the wrackful siege of batt'ring days
When rocks impregnable are not so stout,
Nor gates of steel so strong, but Time decays?
O fearful meditation! Where, alack,
Shall Time's best jewel from Time's chest lie hid,
Or what strong hand can hold his swift foot back,
Or who his spoil of beauty can forbid?
      O, none, unless this miracle have might,
      That in black ink my love may still shine bright.

1 *Since*] since there is neither   2 *o'ersways*] overrules   3 *hold a plea*]
uphold a suit   4 *action*] case at law   6 *wrackful*] destructive; *batt'ring*
days] (like battering rams)   8 *decays*] makes decay   12 *spoil*] ruination

66

Tir'd with all these, for restful death I cry,
As, to behold desert a beggar born,
And needy nothing trimm'd in jollity,
And purest faith unhappily forsworn,
And gilded honour shamefully misplac'd,
And maiden virtue rudely strumpeted,
And right perfection wrongfully disgrac'd,
And strength by limping sway disabled,
And art made tongue-tied by authority,
And folly, doctor-like, controlling skill,
And simple truth miscall'd simplicity,
And captive good attending captain ill:
    Tir'd with all these, from these would I be gone,
    Save that to die I leave my love alone.

2 *As*] as for instance; *desert*] merit   3 *nothing*] worthlessness; *trimm'd in jollity*] dressed up to celebrate   4 *forsworn*] abandoned   5 *gilded*] golden; *shamefully misplac'd*] awarded to the undeserving in shameful manner   6 *strumpeted*] prostituted   8 *limping sway*] halting authority; *disabled*] (four syllables: 'disable-èd')   9 *art*] learning   10 *controlling*] supervising, curbing   14 *to die*] by dying

67

Ah, wherefore with infection should he live
And with his presence grace impiety,
That sin by him advantage should achieve
And lace itself with his society?
Why should false painting imitate his cheek
And steal dead seeming of his living hue?
Why should poor beauty indirectly seek
Roses of shadow, since his rose is true?
Why should he live now Nature bankrupt is,
Beggar'd of blood to blush through lively veins?
For she hath no exchequer now but his,
And 'prov'd of many, lives upon his gains?
    O, him she stores to show what wealth she had
    In days long since, before these last so bad.

1 *with infection*] where infection is   4 *lace*] adorn   5 *false painting*] cosmetics   6 *dead seeming of*] lifeless appearance from   7 *indirectly seek*] deviously seek to realize itself in   8 *Roses of shadow*] illusory beauty (rosy cheeks produced by cosmetics)   9 *bankrupt*] (because she has given all her wealth to the young man)   11 *exchequer*] treasury   12 *'prov'd*] approved (*proud* in 1609); *his gains*] what he has gained (from her)

68

Thus is his cheek the map of days outworn,
When beauty liv'd and died as flowers do now,
Before these bastard signs of fair were borne
Or durst inhabit on a living brow;
Before the golden tresses of the dead,
The right of sepulchres, were shorn away
To live a second life on second head;
Ere beauty's dead fleece made another gay.
In him those holy antique hours are seen
Without all ornament, itself and true,
Making no summer of another's green,
Robbing no old to dress his beauty new;
    And him as for a map doth Nature store,
    To show false Art what beauty was of yore.

1 *outworn*] gone by, worn out of fashion   3 *bastard signs of fair*] low and illegitimate marks of beauty (e.g. the cosmetics of Sonnet 67)   4 *durst inhabit*] (implies assumption of a right when opposed to the passive sense of *were borne*)   6 *The right of sepulchres*] which should have been buried with them   7 *a second life*] (as a wig)   8 *Ere beauty's dead fleece*] before the hair of a dead beauty   9 *antique*] (pronounced 'antic') ancient 11 *of*] out of   13 *store*] keep   14 *false Art*] art that deceives (by use of cosmetics etc.)

69

Those parts of thee that the world's eye doth view
Want nothing that the thought of hearts can mend.
All tongues, the voice of souls, give thee that due,
Utt'ring bare truth even so as foes commend.
Thy outward thus with outward praise is crown'd,
But those same tongues, that give thee so thine own,
In other accents do this praise confound
By seeing farther than the eye hath shown.
They look into the beauty of thy mind,
And that in guess they measure by thy deeds.
Then, churls, their thoughts – although their eyes were kind –
To thy fair flower add the rank smell of weeds:
  But why thy odour matcheth not thy show,
  The soil is this, that thou dost common grow.

2 *Want*] lack   4   *bare*] simple; *even so as*] so that even   6   *thine own*]
what is due to you   7   *accents*] tones; *confound*] destroy   12   *thy fair
flower*] i.e. your beauty   14   *soil*] reason (why the flower is not matched in
beauty by its perfume), stain; *common*] vulgar, cheap, indiscriminate

70

That thou are blam'd shall not be thy defect,
For slander's mark was ever yet the fair;
The ornament of beauty is suspect,
A crow that flies in heaven's sweetest air.
So thou be good, slander doth but approve
Thy worth the greater, being woo'd of time;
For canker vice the sweetest buds doth love,
And thou present'st a pure unstained prime.
Thou hast pass'd by the ambush of young days
Either not assail'd, or victor being charg'd;
Yet this thy praise cannot be so thy praise
To tie up envy, evermore enlarg'd.
     If some suspect of ill mask'd not thy show,
     Then thou alone kingdoms of hearts shouldst owe.

1 *thy defect*] counted to you as a fault (*defect* is stressed on the second syllable)
2 *mark*] target; *fair*] person of beauty   3 Suspicion is worn by beauty like an ornament (*suspect* is stressed on the second syllable here, and l.13)
5 *So*] so long as; *doth but approve*] only demonstrates   6 *woo'd of time*] made much of by Time, subject to the blandishments of the time   7 *canker vice*] vice like a malign grub   8 *prime*] freshness of youth   9 *ambush of young days*] temptations of youth   10 *charg'd*] attacked   11–12 *so ... To tie*] in such a way as to fetter   12 *evermore enlarg'd*] which is always at liberty   13 *suspect*] suspicion   14 *owe*] possess

71

No longer mourn for me when I am dead
Than you shall hear the surly sullen bell
Give warning to the world that I am fled
From this vile world, with vilest worms to dwell.
Nay, if you read this line, remember not
The hand that writ it; for I love you so
That I in your sweet thoughts would be forgot
If thinking on me then should make you woe.
O, if, I say, you look upon this verse
When I perhaps compounded am with clay,
Do not so much as my poor name rehearse,
But let your love even with my life decay,
　　Lest the wise world should look into your moan,
　　And mock you with me after I am gone.

8 *make*] cause　　11 *rehearse*] say over　　13 *moan*] sorrow

72

O, lest the world should task you to recite
What merit liv'd in me that you should love,
After my death, dear love, forget me quite;
For you in me can nothing worthy prove,
Unless you would devise some virtuous lie
To do more for me than mine own desert,
And hang more praise upon deceased I
Than niggard truth would willingly impart.
O, lest your true love may seem false in this,
That you for love speak well of me untrue,
My name be buried where my body is,
And live no more to shame nor me nor you;
    For I am sham'd by that which I bring forth,
    And so should you, to love things nothing worth.

1 *task*] require; *recite*] tell   4 *prove*] discover   6 *desert*] merit
8 *niggard*] miserly; *impart*] give out   10 *untrue*] without truth   11 *My name be*] let my name be   13 *that which I bring forth*] (my verses and plays? your love for me?)   14 *should you*] should you be ashamed

73

That time of year thou mayst in me behold
When yellow leaves, or none, or few, do hang
Upon those boughs which shake against the cold,
Bare ruin'd choirs where late the sweet birds sang.
In me thou seest the twilight of such day
As after sunset fadeth in the west;
Which by and by black night doth take away,
Death's second self, that seals up all in rest.
In me thou seest the glowing of such fire
That on the ashes of his youth doth lie,
As the death-bed whereon it must expire,
Consum'd with that which it was nourish'd by.
    This thou perceiv'st, which makes thy love more strong,
    To love that well which thou must leave ere long.

4 *choirs*] in churches, where divine service is sung   8 *seals up*] (as in a coffin)   10 *his*] its

74

But be contented when that fell arrest
Without all bail shall carry me away.
My life hath in this line some interest,
Which for memorial still with thee shall stay.
When thou reviewest this, thou dost review
The very part was consecrate to thee.
The earth can have but earth, which is his due;
My spirit is thine, the better part of me.
So then thou hast but lost the dregs of life,
The prey of worms, my body being dead,
The coward conquest of a wretch's knife,
Too base of thee to be remembered.
 The worth of that is that which it contains,
 And that is this, and this with thee remains.

1 *fell*] cruel; *arrest*] taking into custody 2 *bail*] possibility of release
3 *line*] (of verse); *interest*] part 4 *memorial*] reminder 6 *part was consecrate*] part that was devoted 7 *his*] its 9 *but*] only 11 *The coward conquest of*] a thing that can in cowardly fashion be conquered by
12 *of*] by 13 The value of the body lies in the spirit it contains 14 *And that is this*] and the spirit is this poetry

75

So are you to my thoughts as food to life,
Or as sweet-season'd showers are to the ground;
And for the peace of you I hold such strife
As 'twixt a miser and his wealth is found,
Now proud as an enjoyer, and anon
Doubting the filching age will steal his treasure;
Now counting best to be with you alone,
Then better'd that the world may see my pleasure;
Sometime all full with feasting on your sight,
And by and by clean starved for a look;
Possessing or pursuing no delight
Save what is had or must from you be took.
    Thus do I pine and surfeit day by day,
    Or gluttoning on all, or all away.

2 *sweet-season'd showers*] temperate showers, showers of the spring   3 *for the peace of you*] for the sake of the peace you bring me, or the peace that you possess   5 *enjoyer*] possessor   6 *Doubting*] fearing; *filching*] thievish   7 *counting*] thinking it   8 *better'd*] thinking it better   10 *clean*] entirely   14 *Or . . . or*] either . . . or; *all away*] having nothing at all

76

Why is my verse so barren of new pride,
So far from variation or quick change?
Why with the time do I not glance aside
To new-found methods and to compounds strange?
Why write I still all one, ever the same,
And keep invention in a noted weed,
That every word doth almost tell my name,
Showing their birth and where they did proceed?
O, know, sweet love, I always write of you,
And you and love are still my argument;
So all my best is dressing old words new,
Spending again what is already spent;
    For as the sun is daily new and old,
    So is my love, still telling what is told.

---

1 *barren of new pride*] lacking in novel ornament   2 *quick*] lively
3 *with the time*] in accordance with fashion   4 *methods*] ways of
proceeding; *compounds strange*] exotic compound phrases   5 *still all one*]
always the same   6 *invention*] poetic subject-matter; *noted weed*] familiar
dress   8 *where*] from where

77

Thy glass will show thee how thy beauties wear,
Thy dial how thy precious minutes waste;
The vacant leaves thy mind's imprint will bear,
And of this book this learning mayst thou taste:
The wrinkles which thy glass will truly show
Of mouthed graves will give thee memory;
Thou by thy dial's shady stealth mayst know
Time's thievish progress to eternity;
Look, what thy memory cannot contain
Commit to these waste blanks, and thou shalt find
Those children nurs'd, deliver'd from thy brain,
To take a new acquaintance of thy mind.
    These offices, so oft as thou wilt look,
    Shall profit thee and much enrich thy book.

1 *glass*] mirror; *wear*] wear away, last out   2 *dial*] sundial; *waste*] pass away   3 The empty pages will bear the traces of your thought (in writing) 4 *this book*] (This poem seems to have accompanied the gift of a blank notebook); *taste*] sample   6 *mouthed*] i.e. wide-mouthed; *give thee memory*] remind you   7 *thy dial's shady stealth*] the stealthy progress of the shadow on your sundial   10 *waste blanks*] blank pages   11 *children*] i.e. your thoughts   13 *offices*] duties (of consulting mirror, sundial and book)

78

So oft have I invok'd thee for my Muse
And found such fair assistance in my verse
As every alien pen hath got my use,
And under thee their poesy disperse.
Thine eyes, that taught the dumb on high to sing
And heavy ignorance aloft to fly,
Have added feathers to the learned's wing
And given grace a double majesty.
Yet be most proud of that which I compile,
Whose influence is thine and born of thee.
In others' works thou dost but mend the style,
And arts with thy sweet graces graced be;
　　　But thou art all my art, and dost advance
　　　As high as learning my rude ignorance.

1 *for*] as   2 *fair*] favourable   3 *As*] that; *alien pen*] pen of a
stranger; *got my use*] adopted my practice   4 *under thee*] in your
service   8 *grace*] excellence; *double majesty*] double claim to admiration
10 *influence*] inspiration (the allusion is to the influence supposed to derive
from stars)   11 *mend*] improve   12 *graced*] beautified   14 *rude*]
simple, crude

79

Whilst I alone did call upon thy aid,
My verse alone had all thy gentle grace;
But now my gracious numbers are decay'd,
And my sick Muse doth give another place.
I grant, sweet love, thy lovely argument
Deserves the travail of a worthier pen,
Yet what of thee thy poet doth invent
He robs thee of, and pays it thee again.
He lends thee virtue, and he stole that word
From thy behaviour; beauty doth he give,
And found it in thy cheek: he can afford
No praise to thee but what in thee doth live.
  Then thank him not for that which he doth say,
  Since what he owes thee thou thyself dost pay.

2 *gentle grace*] courteous favour   3 *numbers*] verses   4 *give another place*] give way to someone else   5 *thy lovely argument*] the subject for writing which you in your loveliness constitute   6 *travail*] labour   7 *invent*] devise   9 *lends*] attributes to   10 *behaviour*] bearing, conduct   14 *what he owes thee*] what it is his duty to pay you

80

O, how I faint when I of you do write,
Knowing a better spirit doth use your name,
And in the praise thereof spends all his might
To make me tongue-tied speaking of your fame!
But since your worth, wide as the ocean is,
The humble as the proudest sail doth bear,
My saucy bark, inferior far to his,
On your broad main doth wilfully appear.
Your shallowest help will hold me up afloat,
Whilst he upon your soundless deep doth ride;
Or, being wreck'd, I am a worthless boat,
He of tall building and of goodly pride.
          Then if he thrive and I be cast away,
          The worst was this: my love was my decay.

1 *faint*] fail in spirit   2 *spirit*] i.e. poet   4 *To make me*] so that I am made   6 *bear*] tolerate, bear up   7 *saucy*] impertinent; *bark*] small boat   8 *main*] ocean; *wilfully*] obstinately   10 *soundless*] unfathomable   11 *being wreck'd*] if either of us is wrecked   12 *tall building*] sturdy construction; *pride*] splendour   14 *my love was my decay*] my love for you, or you whom I love, caused my downfall

81

Or I shall live your epitaph to make,
Or you survive when I in earth am rotten;
From hence your memory death cannot take,
Although in me each part will be forgotten.
Your name from hence immortal life shall have,
Though I, once gone, to all the world must die.
The earth can yield me but a common grave
When you entombed in men's eyes shall lie.
Your monument shall be my gentle verse,
Which eyes not yet created shall o'er-read;
And tongues to be your being shall rehearse
When all the breathers of this world are dead.
        You still shall live – such virtue hath my pen –
        Where breath most breathes, even in the mouths of men.

1-2 *Or ... Or*] Either ... or   3 *hence*] this world, these lines   4 *in me each part*] every quality of mine   5 *from hence*] henceforth, from these lines   6 *to all the world must die*] will be completely dead (there will be no memory of me)   7 *common*] ordinary   8 *entombed in men's eyes*] in a tomb in the sight of all   11 *rehearse*] repeat   13 *virtue*] power

82

I grant thou wert not married to my Muse,
And therefore mayst without attaint o'erlook
The dedicated words which writers use
Of their fair subject, blessing every book.
Thou art as fair in knowledge as in hue,
Finding thy worth a limit past my praise;
And therefore art enforc'd to seek anew
Some fresher stamp of these time-bett'ring days.
And do so, love; yet when they have devis'd
What strained touches rhetoric can lend,
Thou, truly fair, wert truly sympathiz'd
In true plain words by thy true-telling friend;
   And their gross painting might be better us'd
   Where cheeks need blood: in thee it is abus'd.

2 *attaint*] dishonour   3 *dedicated*] devoted; *writers*] i.e. other writers
5 *in knowledge as in hue*] in understanding as in appearance   6 When
you decide that my praise cannot reach the limits of your worth
8 *time-bett'ring days*] days in which the arts are improving on the past
11 *truly sympathiz'd*] given a true likeness   13 *gross painting*] crude
laying on of praise like a cosmetic

83

I never saw that you did painting need,
And therefore to your fair no painting set;
I found, or thought I found, you did exceed
The barren tender of a poet's debt;
And therefore have I slept in your report,
That you yourself, being extant, well might show
How far a modern quill doth come too short,
Speaking of worth, what worth in you doth grow.
This silence for my sin you did impute,
Which shall be most my glory, being dumb;
For I impair not beauty, being mute,
When others would give life, and bring a tomb.
     There lives more life in one of your fair eyes
     Than both your poets can in praise devise.

1 *painting*] (as in the previous sonnet)   2 *fair*] beauty   4 The worthless tribute of poet to patron   5 *slept in your report*] been inactive in publishing your virtues   6 *That*] because; *extant*] in existence   7 *modern*] ordinary, of the present times   9 *for*] as   11 *being mute*] by being silent   14 *both your poets*] the writer and his rival

84

Who is it that says most, which can say more
Than this rich praise, that you alone are you,
In whose confine immured is the store
Which should example where your equal grew?
Lean penury within that pen doth dwell
That to his subject lends not some small glory;
But he that writes of you, if he can tell
That you are you, so dignifies his story.
Let him but copy what in you is writ,
Not making worse what Nature made so clear,
And such a counterpart shall fame his wit,
Making his style admired everywhere.
      You to your beauteous blessings add a curse,
      Being fond on praise, which makes your praises worse.

1 Whoever says most can say no more   3–4 Within whom is confined the abundance of quality which should serve as a model for your equal   8 so] in that way   10 *clear*] without blemish   11 *counterpart*] likeness; *fame his wit*] make his intellectual and creative powers famous   14 *on*] of; *which makes your praises worse*] (because it encourages attempts to improve upon your perfection in praise, and so to diminish it)

85

My tongue-tied Muse in manners holds her still
While comments of your praise, richly compil'd,
Reserve thy character with golden quill
And precious phrase by all the Muses fil'd.
I think good thoughts whilst other write good words,
And like unletter'd clerk still cry 'Amen'
To every hymn that able spirit affords
In polish'd form of well-refined pen.
Hearing you prais'd I say ''Tis so, 'tis true,'
And to the most of praise add something more;
But that is in my thought, whose love to you,
Though words come hindmost, holds his rank before.
 Then others for the breath of words respect,
 Me for my dumb thoughts, speaking in effect.

---

1 *in manners holds her still*] politely keeps silence 2 *comments of your praise*] treatises in your praise 3 *Reserve thy character*] preserve your character (so far that it is reflected in the *character* of their handwriting) 4 *fil'd*] polished 6 *unletter'd*] illiterate 7 *able spirit*] accomplished poet 8 *well-refined pen*] cultivated writer 12 *holds his rank before*] comes first 14 *effect*] deeds

86

Was it the proud full sail of his great verse,
Bound for the prize of all-too-precious you
That did my ripe thoughts in my brain inhearse,
Making their tomb the womb wherein they grew?
Was it his spirit, by spirits taught to write
Above a mortal pitch, that struck me dead?
No, neither he nor his compeers by night
Giving him aid my verse astonished.
He nor that affable familiar ghost
Which nightly gulls him with intelligence,
As victors of my silence cannot boast;
I was not sick of any fear from thence.
　　　But when your countenance fill'd up his line,
　　　Then lack'd I matter; that enfeebled mine.

---

1 *proud*] splendid, arrogant   3 *ripe*] ready for birth; *inhearse*] bury   5 *by spirits taught*] (the spirits that inhabit the great poetry of the past? or literally *spirits*, supernatural beings whom the poet claims to inspire him?)   6 *Above a mortal pitch*] at more than human level   7 *compeers*] associates (either the ancient poets he reads at night or the *spirits* who visit him then)   8 *astonished*] struck dumb   9 *affable familiar ghost*] friendly attendant spirit (*familiar* has sinister undertones)   10 *gulls*] tricks; *intelligence*] superior understanding, privileged information   12 *of*] with   13 *countenance*] face (as subject-matter), approval (of the finished *line*); *fill'd up*] made up for the deficiencies of   14 *matter*] anything to write about

87

Farewell, thou art too dear for my possessing,
And like enough thou know'st thy estimate.
The charter of thy worth gives thee releasing;
My bonds in thee are all determinate.
For how do I hold thee but by thy granting?
And for that riches where is my deserving?
The cause of this fair gift in me is wanting,
And so my patent back again is swerving.
Thyself thou gav'st, thy own worth then not knowing,
Or me to whom thou gav'st it else mistaking;
So thy great gift, upon misprision growing,
Comes home again, on better judgement making.
          Thus have I had thee as a dream doth flatter:
          In sleep a king, but waking no such matter.

---

1 *art too dear*] cost too much in pains, are too much loved by me (and/or others)   2 *estimate*] value   3 *charter of thy worth*] privilege conferred by your high value or creating that value in the eyes of the world; *releasing*] exemption   4 *bonds*] ties (with suggestions of legal contract and of slavery); *determinate*] ended   7 *wanting*] lacking   8 And so my claim to ownership reverts to you   10 *me . . . mistaking*] taking me for other than I was   11 *upon misprision growing*] based on misunderstanding or error

88

When thou shalt be dispos'd to set me light
And place my merit in the eye of scorn,
Upon thy side against myself I'll fight,
And prove thee virtuous though thou art forsworn.
With mine own weakness being best acquainted,
Upon thy part I can set down a story
Of faults conceal'd, wherein I am attainted,
That thou in losing me shall win much glory,
And I by this will be a gainer too;
For bending all my loving thoughts on thee,
The injuries that to myself I do,
Doing thee vantage, double-vantage me.
    Such is my love, to thee I so belong,
    That for thy right myself will bear all wrong.

1   *set me light*] value me little   2   And expose my merits to scorn   6   *Upon thy part*] in your support   7   *attainted*] dishonoured   8   *That*] so that   10   *Bending . . . on*] directing . . . towards   12   Because they benefit you, bring me a double benefit

89

Say that thou didst forsake me for some fault,
And I will comment upon that offence;
Speak of my lameness, and I straight will halt,
Against thy reasons making no defence.
Thou canst not, love, disgrace me half so ill,
To set a form upon desired change,
As I'll myself disgrace, knowing thy will.
I will acquaintance strangle and look strange,
Be absent from thy walks, and in my tongue
Thy sweet beloved name no more shall dwell,
Lest I, too much profane, should do it wrong,
And haply of our old acquaintance tell.
          For thee, against myself I'll vow debate;
          For I must ne'er love him whom thou dost hate.

2 *comment*] expound   3 *halt*] limp   5 *disgrace*] discredit   6 To
offer acceptable reason for the change you wish   8 *acquaintance strangle*]
deny familiarity with you; *strange*] as though I did not know you   9 *thy
walks*] where you pass   11 *too much profane*] too little worthy, so far from
your divine merit   12 *haply*] by chance   13 *vow debate*] promise to
fight

90

Then hate me when thou wilt; if ever, now;
Now, while the world is bent my deeds to cross,
Join with the spite of fortune, make me bow,
And do not drop in for an after-loss.
Ah, do not, when my heart hath scap'd this sorrow,
Come in the rearward of a conquer'd woe;
Give not a windy night a rainy morrow,
To linger out a purpos'd overthrow.
If thou wilt leave me, do not leave me last,
When other petty griefs have done their spite,
But in the onset come; so shall I taste
At first the very worst of fortune's might,
  And other strains of woe, which now seem woe,
  Compar'd with loss of thee will not seem so.

1 *Then*] therefore (following on from Sonnet 89) 4 *drop in for an after-loss*] fall on me as a loss following all the others 5 *scap'd this sorrow*] survived my present trouble 6 *rearward*] rearguard 8 *linger out*] prolong; *purpos'd overthrow*] reversal of fortune intended me 11 *in the onset*] at the start, in the front of the attackers 13 *strains*] kinds

91

Some glory in their birth, some in their skill,
Some in their wealth, some in their body's force,
Some in their garments (though new-fangled ill),
Some in their hawks and hounds, some in their horse;
And every humour hath his adjunct pleasure,
Wherein it finds a joy above the rest.
But these particulars are not my measure;
All these I better in one general best.
Thy love is better than high birth to me,
Richer than wealth, prouder than garments' cost,
Of more delight than hawks or horses be;
And having thee of all men's pride I boast –
    Wretched in this alone, that thou mayst take
    All this away, and me most wretched make.

2 *force*] strength   5 *adjunct*] associated   12 *all men's pride*] all the
things which men take pride in

92

But do thy worst to steal thyself away,
For term of life thou art assured mine,
And life no longer than thy love will stay;
For it depends upon that love of thine.
Then need I not to fear the worst of wrongs
When in the least of them my life hath end.
I see a better state to me belongs
Than that which on thy humour doth depend.
Thou canst not vex me with inconstant mind,
Since that my life on thy revolt doth lie.
O, what a happy title do I find,
Happy to have thy love, happy to die!
　　　But what's so blessed fair that fears no blot?
　　　Thou mayst be false, and yet I know it not.

This follows on from the previous sonnet.　　2　*assured*] pledged　　6　*least of them*] least wrong you can do me　　8　*humour*] mood, caprice　　10　*on thy revolt doth lie*] is at stake if you turn away from me　　11　*title*] claim to possession

93

So shall I live supposing thou art true,
Like a deceived husband; so love's face
May still seem love to me, though alter'd new,
Thy looks with me, thy heart in other place.
For there can live no hatred in thine eye,
Therefore in that I cannot know thy change.
In many's looks the false heart's history
Is writ in moods and frowns and wrinkles strange,
But heaven in thy creation did decree
That in thy face sweet love should ever dwell;
Whate'er thy thoughts or thy heart's workings be,
Thy looks should nothing thence but sweetness tell.
    How like Eve's apple doth thy beauty grow,
    If thy sweet virtue answer not thy show!

This follows on from the previous sonnet.   1 *supposing*] imagining
2 *face*] appearance   7 *many's looks*] the looks of many people

94

They that have power to hurt, and will do none,
That do not do the thing they most do show,
Who, moving others, are themselves as stone,
Unmoved, cold, and to temptation slow –
They rightly do inherit heaven's graces,
And husband nature's riches from expense;
They are the lords and owners of their faces,
Others but stewards of their excellence.
The summer's flower is to the summer sweet,
Though to itself it only live and die,
But if that flower with base infection meet,
The basest weed outbraves his dignity;
            For sweetest things turn sourest by their deeds:
            Lilies that fester smell far worse than weeds.

2 *the thing they most do show*] what they seem most likely to do from
their appearance (some suggestion of hypocrisy, developing as the poem con-
tinues)   5 *rightly*] (ironic tone possible); *graces*] favours (in looks and
otherwise)   6 *husband*] manage prudently; *expense*] being wastefully
expended   8 *stewards*] caretakers, custodians   9 *is to the summer
sweet*] perfumes the summer air   10 *to itself*] in isolation, without reference
to others   11 *base*] loathsome   12 *basest*] lowliest; *outbraves*] sur-
passes (in appearance or moral quality)

95

How sweet and lovely dost thou make the shame
Which, like a canker in the fragrant rose,
Doth spot the beauty of thy budding name!
O, in what sweets dost thou thy sins enclose!
That tongue that tells the story of thy days,
Making lascivious comments on thy sport,
Cannot dispraise, but in a kind of praise,
Naming thy name, blesses an ill report.
O, what a mansion have those vices got
Which for their habitation chose out thee,
Where beauty's veil doth cover every blot,
And all things turns to fair that eyes can see!
    Take heed, dear heart, of this large privilege:
    The hardest knife ill-us'd doth lose his edge.

2 *canker*] grub causing blight   3 *name*] reputation   6 *sport*] (sexual) fun   7–8 The ambiguous punctuation (the two lines may or may not be independent of each other) follows the earliest text   (The subject of *turns* is *beauty, veil*)   14 *his*] its

96

Some say thy fault is youth, some wantonness,
Some say thy grace is youth and gentle sport.
Both grace and faults are lov'd of more and less;
Thou mak'st faults graces that to thee resort.
As on the finger of a thronèd queen
The basest jewel will be well esteem'd,
So are those errors that in thee are seen
To truths translated, and for true things deem'd.
How many lambs might the stern wolf betray
If like a lamb he could his looks translate!
How many gazers mightst thou lead away
If thou wouldst use the strength of all thy state!
  But do not so. I love thee in such sort
  As, thou being mine, mine is thy good report.

1 *wantonness*] playful extravagance, immoral sexuality 2 *gentle*] becoming a gentleman 3 *of more and less*] by all classes of people
8 *translated*] transformed; *deem'd*] judged 9 *betray*] deceive to their misfortune 12 *state*] pre-eminent position 13–14 These lines also conclude Sonnet 36 14 *report*] reputation

97

How like a winter hath my absence been
From thee, the pleasure of the fleeting year!
What freezings have I felt, what dark days seen,
What old December's bareness everywhere!
And yet this time remov'd was summer's time,
The teeming autumn big with rich increase,
Bearing the wanton burden of the prime
Like widow'd wombs after their lords' decease.
Yet this abundant issue seem'd to me
But hope of orphans and unfather'd fruit,
For summer and his pleasures wait on thee,
And thou away, the very birds are mute;
 Or if they sing, 'tis with so dull a cheer
 That leaves look pale, dreading the winter's near.

2 *the pleasure of*] what pleases most in, what is most pleasing to; *fleeting*] swiftly passing   5 *time remov'd*] time of separation; *summer's time*] time for summer to bring forth autumn (as though autumn were summer's child) 6 *teeming*] prolific; *increase*] (stressed on the second syllable)   7 *wanton burden*] i.e. offspring, conceived in pleasure and bringing pleasure; *prime*] spring 11 *his*] its; *wait on*] follow

98

From you have I been absent in the spring
When proud pied April, dress'd in all his trim,
Hath put a spirit of youth in everything,
That heavy Saturn laugh'd and leapt with him.
Yet nor the lays of birds nor the sweet smell
Of different flowers in odour and in hue
Could make me any summer's story tell,
Or from their proud lap pluck them where they grew;
Nor did I wonder at the lily's white,
Nor praise the deep vermilion in the rose.
They were but sweet, but figures of delight
Drawn after you, you pattern of all those;
     Yet seem'd it winter still, and, you away,
     As with your shadow I with these did play.

2 *proud pied*] fine and many-coloured; *trim*] bravery   4 *That*] with the result that; *heavy Saturn*] the ponderous god (and planet) of melancholy   5 *Yet nor the lays*] yet neither the songs   7 *any summer's story tell*] speak cheerfully or of cheerful things   8 *proud*] brilliant; *lap*] i.e. the earth   11 *figures*] secondary representatives   12 *after you*] in your likeness

99

The forward violet thus did I chide:
'Sweet thief, whence didst thou steal thy sweet that smells,
If not from my love's breath? The purple pride
Which on thy soft cheek for complexion dwells
In my love's veins thou hast too grossly dyed.'
The lily I condemned for thy hand,
And buds of marjoram had stol'n thy hair;
The roses fearfully on thorns did stand,
One blushing shame, another white despair.
A third, nor red nor white, had stol'n of both,
And to his robb'ry had annex'd thy breath;
But for his theft in pride of all his growth
A vengeful canker ate him up to death.
    More flowers I noted, yet I none could see
    But sweet or colour it had stol'n from thee.

This poem varies the pattern of the sonnet by adding a line to the normal fourteen. 1 *forward*] precocious, presumptious 3 *purple*] (Not a very specific term of colour in Shakespeare's time); *pride*] splendour 4 *for complexion*] as colouring, as a complexion 5 *grossly*] obviously, shamelessly 6 *for*] for stealing from the whiteness etc. of 7 *marjoram*] thickly-growing herb, sweetly smelling and fair-coloured 8 *fearfully*] anxiously 11 *to his robb'ry had annex'd*] had added to the sum of his thefts 12 *for*] in return for; *pride*] the splendour 13 *canker*] grub causing blight

IOO

Where art thou, Muse, that thou forget'st so long
To speak of that which gives thee all thy might?
Spend'st thou thy fury on some worthless song,
Dark'ning thy power to lend base subjects light?
Return, forgetful Muse, and straight redeem
In gentle numbers time so idly spent;
Sing to the ear that doth thy lays esteem
And gives thy pen both skill and argument.
Rise, resty Muse, my love's sweet face survey
If Time have any wrinkle graven there;
If any, be a satire to decay
And make Time's spoils despised everywhere.
    Give my love fame faster than Time wastes life;
    So, thou preven'st his scythe and crooked knife.

3 *fury*] poetic energy   4 *Dark'ning*] soiling, extinguishing; *base*] unworthy
5 *redeem*] make up for   6 *gentle numbers*] poetry worthy of a gentleman
7 *lays*] songs   8 *argument*] subject-matter   9 *resty*] out of practice
11 *be a satire to*] satirize   12 *spoils*] acts of spoliation   14 *So, thou preven'st*] in that way, you forestall (the verb is 'prevene')

101

O truant Muse, what shall be thy amends
For thy neglect of truth in beauty dyed?
Both truth and beauty on my love depends;
So dost thou too, and therein dignified.
Make answer, Muse. Wilt thou not haply say
Truth needs no colour with his colour fix'd,
Beauty no pencil beauty's truth to lay;
But best is best if never intermix'd'?
Because he needs no praise, wilt thou be dumb?
Excuse not silence so, for 't lies in thee
To make him much outlive a gilded tomb,
And to be prais'd of ages yet to be.
  Then do thy office, Muse; I teach thee how
  To make him seem long hence as he shows now.

2 *truth in beauty dyed*] honesty and fidelity imbued with beauty   3 *depends*]
(Singular verb with plural subject is not uncommon in Shakespeare)   4 *therein
dignified*] are given dignity by that dependence   5 *haply*] perhaps   6 *Truth
needs no colour*] (proverbial); *with his colour fix'd*] in addition to his own
engrained colour   7 *pencil*] fine brush; *lay*] apply   8 *if never intermix'd*] without adulteration   13 *office*] duty   14 *long hence*] a long
time from now

102

My love is strengthen'd, though more weak in seeming.
I love not less, though less the show appear.
That love is merchandiz'd whose rich esteeming
The owner's tongue doth publish everywhere.
Our love was new and then but in the spring
When I was wont to greet it with my lays,
As Philomel in summer's front doth sing,
And stops her pipe in growth of riper days –
Not that the summer is less pleasant now
Than when her mournful hymns did hush the night,
But that wild music burdens every bough,
And sweets grown common lose their dear delight.
 Therefore like her I sometime hold my tongue,
 Because I would not dull you with my song.

3 *rich esteeming*] high valuation 4 *publish*] make public 6 *lays*] songs 7 *Philomel*] the nightingale; *in summer's front*] at the start of summer 8 *her pipe*] her singing; *in growth . . . days*] as summer comes into its own 10 *her*] the nightingale's 14 *dull*] bore, make dull

103

Alack, what poverty my Muse brings forth
That, having such a scope to show her pride,
The argument all bare is of more worth
Than when it hath my added praise beside!
O blame me not if I no more can write:
Look in your glass and there appears a face
That overgoes my blunt invention quite,
Dulling my lines and doing me disgrace.
Were it not sinful then, striving to mend,
To mar the subject that before was well?
For to no other pass my verses tend
Than of your graces and your gifts to tell;
    And more, much more than in my verse can sit,
    Your own glass shows you when you look in it.

2 *pride*] powers, pride in you   3 The unadorned theme is worth more
6 *glass*] mirror   7 *overgoes ... invention*] outstrips my simple, coarse
poetic ability   8 *Dulling*] making dull   9 *mend*] improve   11 *pass*]
purpose

104

To me, fair friend, you never can be old;
For as you were when first your eye I eyed,
Such seems your beauty still. Three winters cold
Have from the forests shook three summers' pride;
Three beauteous springs to yellow autumn turn'd
In process of the seasons have I seen,
Three April perfumes in three hot Junes burn'd
Since first I saw you fresh, which yet are green.
Ah yet doth beauty like a dial-hand
Steal from his figure, and no pace perceiv'd;
So your sweet hue, which methinks still doth stand,
Hath motion, and mine eye may be deceiv'd.
 For fear of which, hear this, thou age unbred:
 Ere you were born was beauty's summer dead.

4 *pride*] fine show 8 *yet*] still; *green*] vigorously youthful 9 *dial-hand*] hand of a clock 10 *Steal*] steal away; *figure*] number on the clock face, bodily form 11 *hue*] complexion; *methinks still doth stand*] seems to me the same as it was, not to change 13 *unbred*] unborn, yet to come

105

Let not my love be call'd idolatry,
Nor my beloved as an idol show,
Since all alike my songs and praises be
To one, of one, still such, and ever so.
Kind is my love today, tomorrow kind,
Still constant in a wondrous excellence.
Therefore my verse, to constancy confin'd,
One thing expressing, leaves out difference.
'Fair, kind, and true' is all my argument,
'Fair, kind, and true' varying to other words,
And in this change is my invention spent,
Three themes in one, which wondrous scope affords.
    Fair, kind, and true have often liv'd alone,
    Which three till now never kept seat in one.

2 *show*] present, appear 4 *still*] always 7 *confin'd*] restricted in subject-matter 8 *leaves out difference*] omits other subjects 9 *argument*] theme 10 Putting 'fair, kind, and true' into other language 11 *change*] transformation-process; *invention*] poetic power

106

When in the chronicle of wasted time
I see descriptions of the fairest wights,
And beauty making beautiful old rhyme
In praise of ladies dead and lovely knights;
Then in the blazon of sweet beauty's best,
Of hand, of foot, of lip, of eye, of brow,
I see their antique pen would have express'd
Even such a beauty as you master now.
So all their praises are but prophecies
Of this our time, all you prefiguring,
And for they look'd but with divining eyes,
They had not skill enough your worth to sing;
  For we which now behold these present days
  Have eyes to wonder, but lack tongues to praise.

1   *wasted*] past, laid waste   2   *wights*] people (archaic in Shakespeare's time)
5   *blazon*] record, memorial (with heraldic associations)   7   *antique*] (stress
on the first syllable)   11   *divining*] forecasting without certainty

107

Not mine own fears, nor the prophetic soul
Of the wide world dreaming on things to come,
Can yet the lease of my true love control,
Suppos'd as forfeit to a confin'd doom.
The mortal moon hath her eclipse endur'd,
And the sad augurs mock their own presage;
Incertainties now crown themselves assur'd,
And peace proclaims olives of endless age.
Now with the drops of this most balmy time
My love looks fresh, and Death to me subscribes,
Since spite of him I'll live in this poor rhyme
While he insults o'er dull and speechless tribes.
 And thou in this shalt find thy monument
 When tyrants' crests and tombs of brass are spent.

This sonnet evidently alludes to events in 'the wide world' – but which? It would not be appropriate here to rehearse the many theories. I take the view that the 'mortal moon' is not the line of battle of the Armada in 1588, nor literally the moon, which underwent an eclipse in 1595, nor anything or anyone else than Queen Elizabeth I, often compared to Diana, goddess of the moon, who experienced her own mortality when she died in 1603 and was replaced by the peace-maker, James I.   1 *prophetic soul*] collective consciousness anxiously anticipating the future   3 *lease*] time allotted; *control*] check, put a limit to   4 Thought subject to termination within an allotted period   6 *sad*] grave, grief-stricken; *mock . . . presage*] are scornful of their own predictions   7 What was uncertain (the succession to Elizabeth?) is no longer so (James will be crowned?)   8 *olives . . . age*] olive branches (symbols of peace) that will last for ever   9 *drops*] tears of joy and grief, medicines; *balmy*] fragrant and healthful   10 *fresh*] young and vigorous; *to me subscribes*] acknowledges me his superior   12 *insults*] triumphs; *speechless*] (because making no rhymes)   14 *spent*] ruined

108

What's in the brain that ink may character
Which hath not figur'd to thee my true spirit?
What's new to speak, what now to register,
That may express my love or thy dear merit?
Nothing, sweet boy; but yet, like prayers divine,
I must each day say o'er the very same,
Counting no old thing old, thou mine, I thine,
Even as when first I hallow'd thy fair name.
So that eternal love in love's fresh case
Weighs not the dust and injury of age,
Nor gives to necessary wrinkles place,
But makes antiquity for aye his page,
    Finding the first conceit of love there bred
    Where time and outward form would show it dead.

1 *character*] put into writing   2 *figur'd*] represented   8 *hallow'd*] blessed   9 *fresh case*] lively state, spruce dress   10 *Weighs not*] takes no account of   12 But makes of age his ever-young servant   13 *first conceit of love*] love in its original force   14 *would show it*] make it appear, wish it to appear

109

O never say that I was false of heart,
Though absence seem'd my flame to qualify.
As easy might I from myself depart
As from my soul, which in thy breast doth lie;
That is my home of love. If I have rang'd,
Like him that travels, I return again,
Just to the time, not with the time exchang'd,
So that myself bring water for my stain.
Never believe, though in my nature reign'd
All frailties that besiege all kinds of blood,
That it could so preposterously be stain'd
To leave for nothing all thy sum of good;
    For nothing this wide universe I call,
    Save thou, my rose; in it thou art my all.

2 *my flame to qualify*] to diminish my love for you   5 *rang'd*] wandered
7 True to my appointed hour and not changed by the passage of time
10 *kinds of blood*] i.e. temperaments   11 *preposterously*] unnaturally

110

Alas, 'tis true, I have gone here and there
And made myself a motley to the view,
Gor'd mine own thoughts, sold cheap what is most dear,
Made old offences of affections new.
Most true it is that I have look'd on truth
Askance and strangely; but, by all above,
These blenches gave my heart another youth,
And worse essays prov'd thee my best of love.
Now all is done, have what shall have no end:
Mine appetite I never more will grind
On newer proof, to try an older friend,
A god in love, to whom I am confin'd.
    Then give me welcome, next my heaven the best,
    Even to thy pure and most most loving breast.

2 *a motley to the view*] visibly a fool ('motley' is the characteristic dress of fools)   3 *Gor'd*] wounded, tricked out in 'gores' (the triangular pieces of cloth that are part of 'motley')   4 Given new instances of my old offence of unfaithfulness   6 *strangely*] as though without recognition   7 *blenches*] ?foolish tricks (a very difficult word to gloss, apparently combining ideas of trickery and game with that of a feint or swerve from the direct line) 8 *worse essays*] experience of an inferior love   10 *grind*] whet, sharpen 11 *On newer proof*] by experiment with the new   12 *confin'd*] bound 13 *next my heaven the best*] the best welcome, next to you, my heaven

111

O, for my sake do you with Fortune chide,
The guilty goddess of my harmful deeds,
That did not better for my life provide
Than public means which public manners breeds.
Thence comes it that my name receives a brand,
And almost thence my nature is subdu'd
To what it works in, like the dyer's hand.
Pity me then, and wish I were renew'd,
Whilst, like a willing patient, I will drink
Potions of eisel 'gainst my strong infection;
No bitterness that I will bitter think,
Nor double penance to correct correction.
      Pity me then, dear friend, and I assure ye
      Even that your pity is enough to cure me.

2 *guilty*] (Fortune shares in the guilt of the deeds she encouraged)   3 *life*] livelihood   4 *public means*] a living made in the public world; *public manners breeds*] generates vulgar, showy behaviour   5 *brand*] stigma 6–7 *subdu'd/ To*] overpowered by   10 *eisel*] vinegar (taken against the plague)   11 *No bitterness*] There is no bitterness   12 *to correct correction*] to correct further what has been corrected already by a first penance

112

Your love and pity doth th'impression fill
Which vulgar scandal stamp'd upon my brow;
For what care I who calls me well or ill,
So you o'er-green my bad, my good allow?
You are my all the world, and I must strive
To know my shames and praises from your tongue;
None else to me, nor I to none alive,
That my steel'd sense or changes right or wrong.
In so profound abysm I throw all care
Of others' voices that my adder's sense
To critic and to flatterer stopped are.
Mark how with my neglect I do dispense:
    You are so strongly in my purpose bred
    That all the world besides, methinks th'are dead.

1 *impression*] i.e. scar (cf. the *brand* of the previous sonnet)   2 *vulgar scandal*] public disgrace, common slander; *stamp'd*] i.e. branded   4 *o'er-green*] cover with fresh and healthy growth; *allow*] approve   7–8 There is no one else alive who matters for me, or to whom I matter, who affects my obdurate sense, for right or wrong   9 *In so profound*] into so deep an   10 *adder's sense*] (The adder was proverbially deaf)   12 *with ... dispense*] I excuse my neglect (of others' voices)   13 *in my purpose bred*] cherished in and by my committed self   14 *th'are*] they (i.e. all the world besides) are

113

Since I left you, mine eye is in my mind,
And that which governs me to go about
Doth part his function and is partly blind,
Seems seeing, but effectually is out;
For it no form delivers to the heart
Of bird, of flower, or shape which it doth latch:
Of his quick objects hath the mind no part,
Nor his own vision holds what it doth catch;
For if it see the rud'st or gentlest sight,
The most sweet-favour or deformed'st creature,
The mountain or the sea, the day or night,
The crow or dove, it shapes them to your feature.
    Incapable of more, replete with you,
    My most true mind thus mak'th mine eye untrue.

3 *Doth . . . function*] partly does its job   4 *effectually*] effectively; *out*] off
the mark, defunct   6 *latch*] apprehend   7 *his*] its (the sight's); *quick*]
fleeting, lively   10 *sweet-favour*] i.e. sweet-favoured   13 *incapable of*]
unable to take in

114

Or whether doth my mind, being crown'd with you,
Drink up the monarch's plague, this flattery?
Or whether shall I say mine eye saith true,
And that your love taught it this alchemy,
To make of monsters and things indigest
Such cherubins as your sweet self resemble,
Creating every bad a perfect best
As fast as objects to his beams assemble?
O, 'tis the first, 'tis flattery in my seeing,
And my great mind most kingly drinks it up.
Mine eye well knows what with his gust is 'greeing,
And to his palate doth prepare the cup.
    If it be poison'd, 'tis the lesser sin
    That mine eye loves it and doth first begin.

1, 3   *Or whether . . . Or whether*] (indicates alternative questions)   1   *crown'd with you*] made a king by your love   5   *indigest*] shapeless   8   As fast as objects come within my gaze   9   *flattery*] (2 syllables here, though 3 in line 2)   10   *most kingly*] in perfect royal fashion   11   *what with . . . 'greeing*] what is to my mind's taste   12   *to*] to please   14   *doth first begin*] drinks first

115

Those lines that I before have writ do lie,
Even those that said I could not love you dearer;
Yet then my judgement knew no reason why
My most full flame should afterwards burn clearer.
But reckoning Time, whose million'd accidents
Creep in 'twixt vows and change decrees of kings,
Tan sacred beauty, blunt the sharp'st intents,
Divert strong minds to th'course of alt'ring things –
Alas, why, fearing of Time's tyranny,
Might I not then say 'Now I love you best',
When I was certain o'er incertainty,
Crowning the present, doubting of the rest?
    Love is a babe; then might I not say so,
    To give full growth to that which still doth grow.

---

5 *accidents*] occurrences   7 *Tan*] darken, turn leathery   8 *course*] way (here, perhaps with the suggestion of a water-course)   11 *o'er incertainty*] despite others' doubts, despite my own doubts about the future, despite the uncertain nature of the world   12 *Crowning the present*] making the present a royal time, treating it as though it were   13 *babe*] (because Cupid is so depicted); *then*] therefore, at that time   14 Because it suggested that my love, which is still growing, had reached its fullest maturity

116

Let me not to the marriage of true minds
Admit impediments. Love is not love
Which alters when it alteration finds,
Or bends with the remover to remove.
O no, it is an ever-fixed mark
That looks on tempests and is never shaken;
It is the star to every wand'ring bark,
Whose worth's unknown although his height be taken.
Love's not Time's fool, though rosy lips and cheeks
Within his bending sickle's compass come;
Love alters not with his brief hours and weeks,
But bears it out even to the edge of doom.
  If this be error and upon me prov'd,
  I never writ, nor no man ever lov'd.

2 *Admit*] allow consideration of   3-4 That changes when it discovers
change (in the appearance or affections of the loved one), or alters course if the
loved one turns elsewhere   5 *mark*] sea-mark (here, a star by which
bearings are to be taken)   7 *bark*] boat   8 *worth*] value, quality (and
hence, perhaps, true nature); *his . . . taken*] its altitude be measured (the height
of the pole star being an indication of latitude, and so an indication of where a
boat is)   9 *Time's fool*] made a mock of by Time   12 *bears it out*]
endures; *edge of doom*] judgement-day

117

Accuse me thus: that I have scanted all
Wherein I should your great deserts repay,
Forgot upon your dearest love to call,
Whereto all bonds do tie me day by day;
That I have frequent been with unknown minds,
And given to time your own dear-purchas'd right;
That I have hoisted sail to all the winds
Which should transport me farthest from your sight.
Book both my wilfulness and errors down,
And on just proof surmise accumulate;
Bring me within the level of your frown,
But shoot not at me in your waken'd hate,
      Since my appeal says I did strive to prove
      The constancy and virtue of your love.

---

1 *scanted*] given short measure in   2 *great deserts*] many and excellent qualities deserving of my love   5 *frequent*] familiar; *unknown minds*] strangers, people unknown to you, of no significance   6 *given ... right*] wasted the time which was yours by virtue of your dearest love   9 *Book ... down*] put on record   10 *on just ... accumulate*] add what you suspect to what you have certain proof of   11 *level*] aim (as of a weapon)   13 *appeal*] plea (in mitigation); *prove*] test

118

Like as, to make our appetites more keen,
With eager compounds we our palate urge;
As, to prevent our maladies unseen,
We sicken to shun sickness when we purge;
Even so, being full of your ne'er-cloying sweetness,
To bitter sauces did I frame my feeding;
And, sick of welfare, found a kind of meetness
To be diseas'd ere that there was true needing.
Thus policy in love, t' anticipate
The ills that were not, grew to faults assur'd,
And brought to medicine a healthful state
Which, rank of goodness, would by ill be cur'd.
    But thence I learn, and find the lesson true:
    Drugs poison him that so fell sick of you.

1 *Like as*] just as   2 *eager compounds*] sharp sauces or medicinal mixtures; *urge*] stimulate   3 *prevent*] forestall; *unseen*] not yet detected   4 *sicken*] make ourselves ill; *purge*] take laxative medicine   6 *frame my feeding*] direct my diet   7 *welfare*] health   9 *policy*] cunning, (mistaken) prudence   10 *grew to faults assur'd*] developed indubitable illness   11 *medicine*] i.e. need of medicine   12 *rank of*] surfeited with

119

What potions have I drunk of siren tears
Distill'd from limbecks foul as hell within,
Applying fears to hopes and hopes to fears,
Still losing when I saw myself to win!
What wretched errors hath my heart committed
Whilst it hath thought itself so blessed never!
How have mine eyes out of their spheres been fitted
In the distraction of this madding fever!
O benefit of ill! Now I find true
That better is by evil still made better,
And ruin'd love when it is built anew
Grows fairer than at first, more strong, far greater.
  So I return rebuk'd to my content,
  And gain by ills thrice more than I have spent.

---

1 *potions*] medicinal draughts; *siren*] alluring   2 *limbecks*] alembics, stills
3 *Applying*] (as 'potions' are applied to sicknesses)   6 *so blessed never*]
happy as never before   7 *spheres*] sockets; *fitted*] driven by fits   8 *of
this madding fever*] caused by the fever of this madness   9 *ill*] sickness,
doing wrong   13 *to my content*] (return) to what makes me happy,
(rebuked) in a way that pleases me (from its outcome)

120

That you were once unkind befriends me now,
And for that sorrow which I then did feel
Needs must I under my transgression bow,
Unless my nerves were brass or hammer'd steel.
For if you were by my unkindness shaken
As I by yours, y'have pass'd a hell of time,
And I, a tyrant, have no leisure taken
To weigh how once I suffer'd in your crime.
O that our night of woe might have remember'd
My deepest sense how hard true sorrow hits,
And soon to you, as you to me then, tender'd
The humble salve which wounded bosoms fits!
    But that your trespass now becomes a fee;
    Mine ransoms yours, and yours must ransom me.

2 *for*] on account of   3 *under my transgression bow*] submit to a sense of my own wrong-doing   4 *nerves*] sinews, feelings   7–8 *have no . . . weigh*] have not taken the time to reflect   8 *in your crime*] at your wrong behaviour to me   9 *night of woe*] dark time of sorrow; *remember'd*] brought back to mind   11 And that I had speedily offered to you, as you did to me then   12 *humble salve*] remedy of humility, simple remedy; *bosoms*] i.e. hearts   13 *your trespass*] the wrong you did; *fee*] payment, reward   14 *ransoms . . . ransom*] pays for . . . redeem

121

'Tis better to be vile than vile esteem'd,
When not to be receives reproach of being,
And the just pleasure lost, which is so deem'd
Not by our feeling but by others' seeing.
For why should others' false adulterate eyes
Give salutation to my sportive blood?
Or on my frailties why are frailer spies,
Which in their wills count bad what I think good?
No, I am that I am, and they that level
At my abuses reckon up their own;
I may be straight, though they themselves be bevel –
By their rank thoughts my deeds must not be shown,
    Unless this general evil they maintain:
    All men are bad and in their badness reign.

2 *not to be*] i.e. not being vile   3 *just*] legitimate, honourable; *so deem'd*] judged to be vile   5 *adulterate*] impure   6 Greet with familiarity (the actions of) my impetuously expressive love (the line is especially difficult to gloss – there is a suggestion of unpleasantly knowing looks from the 'adulterate eyes', and 'sportive' hovers between ideas of innocent play and guilty sexuality)   7 *why are*] why are there set   8 *wills*] conduct of the will, wilfulness   9 *level*] guess, aim (as with a weapon)   10 *abuses*] misdeeds   11 *bevel*] not straight, at a slant   12 *By*] by analogy with; *rank*] lustful, coarse   14 *in their badness reign*] are royal in nature despite their badness, succeed by being bad

122

Thy gift, thy tables, are within my brain
Full character'd with lasting memory,
Which shall above that idle rank remain
Beyond all date, even to eternity –
Or at the least so long as brain and heart
Have faculty by nature to subsist;
Till each to raz'd oblivion yield his part
Of thee, thy record never can be miss'd.
That poor retention could not so much hold,
Nor need I tallies thy dear love to score;
Therefore to give them from me was I bold,
To trust those tables that receive thee more.
        To keep an adjunct to remember thee
        Were to import forgetfulness in me.

1 *thy tables*] your notebooks (apparently containing the friend's notes)
2 *Full character'd*] completely inscribed (describing both the 'tables' and
their impression 'within my brain')   3 *idle rank*] trivial list (of notes)
4 *date*] foreseeable time   6 *Have faculty*] are permitted   7 *raz'd*]
blank   9 *That poor retention*] i.e. 'thy tables'   10 *tallies ... to score*]
crude recording devices ... to mark up   12 *those ... more*] i.e. my own
'brain and heart'   13 *adjunct*] aid   14 *import*] imply

123

No, Time, thou shalt not boast that I do change;
Thy pyramids built up with newer might
To me are nothing novel, nothing strange;
They are but dressings of a former sight.
Our dates are brief, and therefore we admire
What thou dost foist upon us that is old,
And rather make them born to our desire
Than think that we before have heard them told.
Thy registers and thee I both defy,
Not wond'ring at the present nor the past;
For thy records and what we see doth lie,
Made more or less by thy continual haste.
    This I do vow, and this shall ever be:
    I will be true despite thy scythe and thee.

2 *pyramids*] great structures; *newer might*] new force   4 *dressings of*] elaborations on   5 *Our dates*] period of time allowed us   7 *make ... desire*] imagine them new because we want them to be so   9 *registers*] chronicles   11 *doth lie*] i.e. do lie   12 *more or less*] i.e. more or less significant; *by*] as a result of

124

If my dear love were but the child of state,
It might for Fortune's bastard be unfather'd,
As subject to Time's love or to Time's hate,
Weeds among weeds or flowers with flowers gather'd.
No, it was builded far from accident
It suffers not in smiling pomp, nor falls
Under the blow of thralled discontent
Whereto th'inviting time our fashion calls.
It fears not Policy, that heretic,
Which works on leases of short-numbered hours,
But all alone stands hugely politic,
That it nor grows with heat nor drowns with showers.
　　　To this I witness call the fools of Time,
　　　Which die for goodness, who have lived for crime.

1 *my dear love*] my precious love for the friend; *child of state*] product of
circumstance, of his (glamorous) high position   2 *unfather'd*] denied its
true paternity, disowned (and made out to be illegitimate offspring)   3 *As*]
because   5 *accident*] (the domain of) chance   7 *thralled discontent*]
the misery arising from service, from servitude   8 Which the fashion of the
times makes attractive to us   9 *Policy*] expediency   10 *on ... hours*]
for and with short-term interests   11 *hugely politic*] massively sagacious
12 *That*] in that; *nor ... nor*] neither ... nor   13 *fools of Time*] those
who make themselves fools by following the whims of the time, time-servers
14 Who, having lived badly, only manage to do good by dying

125

Were't aught to me I bore the canopy,
With my extern the outward honouring,
Or laid great bases for eternity
Which proves more short than waste or ruining?
Have I not seen dwellers on form and favour
Lose all and more by paying too much rent,
For compound sweet forgoing simple savour,
Pitiful thrivers in their gazing spent?
No, let me be obsequious in thy heart,
And take thou my oblation, poor but free,
Which is not mix'd with seconds, knows no art
But mutual render, only me for thee.
     Hence, thou suborn'd informer! A true soul
     When most impeach'd stands least in thy control.

---

1 *Were't aught*] Would it be anything; *bore the canopy*] (in the procession of some great person)   2 *extern*] outward bearing; *outward*] public aspect (of the great person, of affairs)   3 *laid . . . eternity*] made great preparations for enduring achievement   4 Which turns out not to endure as long as decay and destruction   5 *dwellers on*] sticklers for   8 Wretched men though they prosper, used up in feeding their eyes   9 *be obsequious*] offer my service   10 *oblation*] offering; *free*] freely given   11 *mix'd with seconds*] adulterated (the offering is unqualified); *art*] artifice, trickery   12 *But mutual render*] But is the offering up of one to the other and *vice versa*   13 *thou suborn'd informer*] (you who pretend that I am attracted by outward things and who are yourself corrupted, a hired spy)   14 *impeach'd*] accused; *control*] power

126

O thou my lovely boy, who in thy power
Dost hold Time's fickle glass, his sickle hour,
Who hast by waning grown, and therein
　　show'st
Thy lovers withering as thy sweet self grow'st –
If Nature, sovereign mistress over wrack,
As thou goest onwards still will pluck thee back,
She keeps thee to this purpose, that her skill
May Time disgrace, and wretched minutes kill.
Yet fear her, O thou minion of her pleasure!
She may detain but not still keep her treasure.
Her audit, though delay'd, answer'd must be,
And her quietus is to render thee.

Not a defective sonnet, though it is printed like one in the Quarto of 1609, which marks off the 'missing' lines 13 and 14 with brackets; rather, an envoy in six couplets concluding the sequence of sonnets about the friend. 1 *lovely*] beautiful, arousing love 2 *glass*] hour-glass; *sickle hour*] hour that cuts down human life 3 *waning*] growing older (by losing years from his allotted span) 4 *lovers*] (possibly 'lover's') 5 *wrack*] decay 6 *onwards*] (to death); *still*] always, continually 7 *to*] with 8 *disgrace*] dishonour; *kill*] put an end to (the triumph of) 9 *minion*] darling 10 *still*] for ever 11 *audit*] final reckoning; *answer'd*] made 14 *quietus*] discharge

127

In the old age black was not counted fair,
Or if it were, it bore not beauty's name;
But now is black beauty's successive heir,
And beauty slander'd with a bastard shame:
For since each hand hath put on nature's power,
Fairing the foul with art's false borrow'd face,
Sweet beauty hath no name, no holy bower,
But is profan'd, if not lives in disgrace.
Therefore my mistress' eyes are raven-black,
Her brow so suited, and they mourners seem
At such who, not born fair, no beauty lack,
Sland'ring creation with a false esteem.
  Yet so they mourn, becoming of their woe,
  That every tongue says beauty should look so.

1 *age*] days; *fair*] beautiful, not dark   3 *successive*] i.e. legitimate
4 *slander'd . . . shame*] spoken ill of as illegitimate   5 *put on nature's
power*] usurped nature's authority   6 *Fairing the foul*] making the ugly
beautiful; *art's false borrow'd face*] cosmetics   7 *holy bower*] place where
it is reverenced   10 *so suited*] similarly dressed (in black)   11 *no
beauty lack*] (because they cheat by using cosmetics)   12 Giving nature a
bad name by the false judgments to which they give rise   13 *becoming of*]
giving grace to

128

How oft, when thou, my music, music play'st
Upon that blessed wood whose motion sounds
With thy sweet fingers when thou gently sway'st
The wiry concord that mine ear confounds,
Do I envy those jacks that nimble leap
To kiss the tender inward of thy hand,
Whilst my poor lips, which should that harvest reap,
At the wood's boldness by thee blushing stand!
To be so tickled they would change their state
And situation with those dancing chips
O'er whom thy fingers walk with gentle gait,
Making dead wood more bless'd than living lips.
    Since saucy jacks so happy are in this,
    Give them thy fingers, me thy lips to kiss.

---

1 *thou, my music*] you who are yourself music to me   2 *wood*] (of the virginals, a keyboard instrument); *motion*] movement   3 *sway'st*] command 4 *wiry concord*] harmony of the strings   5 *jacks*] keys (strictly speaking the 'jack' is what plucks the string of the instrument), low fellows   8 *by thee*] beside you   9 *they*] i.e. my lips; *state*] nature   10 *chips*] (of wood: the keys of the virginals)

129

Th'expense of spirit in a waste of shame
Is lust in action; and till action, lust
Is perjur'd, murd'rous, bloody, full of blame,
Savage, extreme, rude, cruel, not to trust,
Enjoy'd no sooner but despised straight,
Past reason hunted, and no sooner had
Past reason hated as a swallowed bait
On purpose laid to make the taker mad;
Mad in pursuit and in possession so,
Had, having, and in quest to have, extreme;
A bliss in proof and prov'd, a very woe;
Before, a joy propos'd; behind, a dream.
    All this the world well knows, yet none knows well
    To shun the heaven that leads men to this hell.

1 *expense*] using up, paying out; *in a waste of shame*] in the course of shameful extravagance, in a wasteland created by shame   3 *perjur'd*] lying; *full of blame*] greatly to be blamed, very ready to blame (others)   4 *not to trust*] not to be trusted   7 *bait*] (like a rat-poison)   9 *Mad*] (Possibly should be 'Made', as in the 1609 Quarto – i.e. 'made . . . extreme')   11 *in proof*] in the experiencing; *prov'd*] once experienced

130

My mistress' eyes are nothing like the sun;
Coral is far more red than her lips' red.
If snow be white, why then her breasts are dun;
If hairs be wires, black wires grow on her head.
I have seen roses damask'd, red and white,
But no such roses see I in her cheeks;
And in some perfumes is there more delight
Than in the breath that from my mistress reeks.
I love to hear her speak, yet well I know
That music hath a far more pleasing sound.
I grant I never saw a goddess go:
My mistress when she walks treads on the ground.
    And yet, by heaven, I think my love as rare
    As any she belied with false compare.

3 *dun*] dull greyish-brown   5 *damask'd*] i.e. mingling red and white
8 *reeks*] breathes (apparently without the modern sense of a foul smell)
11 *go*] walk   14 *belied*] made the subject of untruth; *false compare*]
misleading, deceiving comparison

131

Thou art as tyrannous, so as thou art,
As those whose beauties proudly make them cruel,
For well thou know'st to my dear doting heart
Thou art the fairest and most precious jewel.
Yet, in good faith, some say that thee behold,
Thy face hath not the power to make love groan.
To say they err I dare not be so bold,
Although I swear it to myself alone.
And, to be sure that is not false I swear,
A thousand groans, but thinking on thy face,
One on another's neck, do witness bear
Thy black is fairest in my judgement's place.
    In nothing art thou black save in thy deeds,
    And thence this slander, as I think, proceeds.

1 *so as thou art*] such as you are (i.e. not conventionally 'fair', being 'black')
5 *that thee behold*] who see you   8 *alone*] only, in private   9 *that . . .
swear*] that what I swear is not untrue   11 *One*] i.e. one groan   12 *in
my judgement's place*] in the place given to it by my judgement   14 *this
slander*] (that you are a tyrant)

132

Thine eyes I love, and they, as pitying me,
Knowing thy heart torment me with disdain,
Have put on black, and loving mourners be,
Looking with pretty ruth upon my pain;
And truly, not the morning sun of heaven
Better becomes the grey cheeks of the east,
Nor that full star that ushers in the even
Doth half that glory to the sober west,
As those two mourning eyes become thy face.
O, let it then as well beseem thy heart
To mourn for me, since mourning doth thee grace,
And suit thy pity like in every part.
    Then will I swear Beauty herself is black,
    And all they foul that thy complexion lack.

2 *torment*] torments   4 *ruth*] pity   7 *that full star*] Hesperus, the evening star   8 *Doth*] gives; *sober*] grey, soberly dressed   10 *beseem*] be fitting for (the word would have sounded archaic even in Shakespeare's time)   12 *suit . . . like*] dress the same, make consistent   14 *foul*] ugly

133

Beshrew that heart that makes my heart to groan
For that deep wound it gives my friend and me!
Is 't not enough to torture me alone,
But slave to slavery my sweet'st friend must be?
Me from myself thy cruel eye hath taken,
And my next self thou harder hast engross'd.
Of him, myself, and thee I am forsaken;
A torment thrice threefold thus to be cross'd.
Prison my heart in thy steel bosom's ward,
But then my friend's heart let my poor heart bail;
Whoe'er keeps me, let my heart be his guard;
Thou canst not then use rigour in my jail.
            And yet thou wilt; for I, being pent in thee,
            Perforce am thine, and all that is in me.

---

1 *Beshrew*] (a mild curse)   2 *For*] on account of   3 *alone*] only
4 *slave to slavery*] enslaved to love (which is itself slavery)   6 *my next self*] my second self, my friend; *harder*] more cruelly; *engross'd*] taken exclusive possession of   8 *cross'd*] frustrated   9 *Prison*] imprison; *ward*] cell
10 *bail*] take responsibility for   12 *use rigour*] exercise cruelty; *my jail*] i.e. my heart, where I guard my friend   13 *pent*] imprisoned

134

So, now I have confess'd that he is thine,
And I myself am mortgag'd to thy will,
Myself I'll forfeit, so that other mine
Thou wilt restore to be my comfort still.
But thou wilt not, nor he will not be free,
For thou art covetous, and he is kind.
He learn'd but surety-like to write for me
Under that bond that him as fast doth bind.
The statute of thy beauty thou wilt take,
Thou usurer that put'st forth all to use,
And sue a friend came debtor for my sake;
So him I lose through my unkind abuse.
      Him have I lost; thou hast both him and me;
      He pays the whole, and yet am I not free.

2 *mortgag'd*] pledged; *to thy will*] to (serve) your will, your sexual appetite
3 *that other mine*] i.e. my friend   4 *restore*] return; *still*] always   5 *nor*]
and   6 *covetous*] greedy; *kind*] generous   7 *surety-like ... me*] to sign
his name as a guarantor on my behalf   9 *statute*] all the dues to which your
beauty entitles you   10 *that ... use*] i.e. that have nothing on which you
do not seek a return   11 *came*] who became   12 *abuse*] of my friend
by my loving you, of me by you

135

Whoever hath her wish, thou hast thy will,
And will to boot, and will in overplus.
More than enough am I that vex thee still,
To thy sweet will making addition thus.
Wilt thou, whose will is large and spacious,
Not once vouchsafe to hide my will in thine?
Shall will in others seem right gracious,
And in my will no fair acceptance shine?
The sea, all water, yet receives rain still,
And in abundance addeth to his store;
So thou, being rich in will, add to thy will
One will of mine to make thy large will more.
    Let no unkind 'no' fair beseechers kill;
    Think all but one, and me in that one will.

---

1 *thy will*] (The 1609 quarto capitalizes and italicizes this word more often than not in this sonnet and the next one. A pun is certainly implied on the name Will; the word also means desire, both generally and sexually, and stands for the sexual parts both male and female)   4 *making addition thus*] (by being 'in overplus')   6 *vouchsafe*] consent   8 *in my will*] in the case of what I want   11 *in will*] in being strong-willed, in having Will as your suitor 11–12 *add . . . will more*] add to what you purpose one wish of mine to extend your capacious desire as far as me   13–14 Let no hurtful refusal kill those who ask you politely, who are handsome, honest suitors; imagine all your suitors one man, and give me a place in him, in his desire, in your desire for him

136

If thy soul check thee that I come so near,
Swear to thy blind soul that I was thy Will,
And will, thy soul knows, is admitted there;
Thus far for love my love-suit, sweet, fulfil.
Will will fulfil the treasure of thy love,
Ay, fill it full with Wills, and my will one.
In things of great receipt with ease we prove
Among a number one is reckon'd none.
Then in the number let me pass untold,
Though in thy store's account I one must be;
For nothing hold me, so it please thee hold
That nothing me a something, sweet, to thee.
    Make but my name thy love, and love that still,
    And then thou lov'st me, for my name is Will.

1   *check*] rebuke   5   *fulfil the treasure*] fill the treasury   7   *things of great receipt*] large financial matters, women's sexual parts that receive many men   8   *Among a number*] where the number is large   9   *untold*] uncounted, unnoticed   10   *thy store's account*] the list of what you own   11–12   Think me a nothing so long as you hold that nothing, me, as something special to you (The joke lies in the pun on 'thing' as 'penis')

137

Thou blind fool, Love, what dost thou to mine eyes,
That they behold and see not what they see?
They know what beauty is, see where it lies,
Yet what the best is take the worst to be.
If eyes corrupt by over-partial looks
Be anchor'd in the bay where all men ride,
Why of eyes' falsehood hast thou forged hooks,
Whereto the judgement of my heart is tied?
Why should my heart think that a several plot
Which my heart knows the wide world's common place?
Or mine eyes, seeing this, say this is not,
To put fair truth upon so foul a face?
>   In things right true my heart and eyes have err'd,
>   And to this false plague are they now transferr'd.

1 *Thou blind fool*] (Love is proverbially blind)　　3 *lies*] lives　　5 *corrupt*] corrupted; *over-partial*] prejudiced to excess　　6 Be fixed on the woman who is enjoyed by all men　　7 *of eyes' falsehood*] out of the vision of deceiving eyes　　9 *that a several plot*] that place a private patch of ground 10 *common place*] open land (with a pun on 'common' as 'promiscuous' 12 *To put*] so as to put　　14 *false plague*] plague of seeing false, false woman who plagues me

138

When my love swears that she is made of truth,
I do believe her, though I know she lies,
That she might think me some untutor'd youth
Unlearned in the world's false subtleties.
Thus vainly thinking that she thinks me young,
Although she knows my days are past the best,
Simply I credit her false-speaking tongue;
On both sides thus is simple truth suppress'd.
But wherefore says she not she is unjust?
And wherefore say not I that I am old?
O, love's best habit is in seeming trust,
And age in love loves not to have years told.
   Therefore I lie with her, and she with me,
   And in our faults by lies we flatter'd be.

1 *truth*] faithfulness   7 *Simply*] straightforwardly, like a simpleton; *credit*]
believe   11 *habit*] way of behaving, dress   12 *told*] counted   13 *lie
with*] lie to, make love with   14 *faults*] shortcomings, weakness

139

O, call not me to justify the wrong
That thy unkindness lays upon my heart;
Wound me not with thine eye but with thy tongue;
Use power with power, and slay me not by art.
Tell me thou lov'st elsewhere, but in my sight,
Dear heart, forbear to glance thine eye aside:
What need'st thou wound with cunning when thy might
Is more than my o'erpress'd defence can bide?
Let me excuse thee: 'Ah, my love well knows
Her pretty looks have been mine enemies,
And therefore from my face she turns my foes,
That they elsewhere might dart their injuries.'
  Yet do not so; but since I am near slain,
  Kill me outright with looks, and rid my pain.

2   That you do to me in being unkind to my love for you   3   Do not hurt
me by the way you look (kindly at other people) but by talking out to me
4   *Power with power*] your power (over me) powerfully; *art*] subterfuge
6   *aside*] (at others)   8   *o'erpress'd*] too hard-pressed; *bide*] withstand
10   *mine enemies*] (by wounding me with their beauty, so that I have the
misfortune to love her)   14   *rid*] do away with

140

Be wise as thou art cruel; do not press
My tongue-tied patience with too much disdain,
Lest sorrow lend me words, and words express
The manner of my pity-wanting pain.
If I might teach thee wit, better it were,
Though not to love, yet, love, to tell me so,
As testy sick men, when their deaths be near,
No news but health from their physicians know.
For if I should despair, I should grow mad,
And in my madness might speak ill of thee;
Now this ill-wresting world is grown so bad
Mad sland'rers by mad ears believed be.
  That I may not be so, nor thou belied,
    Bear thine eyes straight, though thy proud
       heart go wide.

1 *press*] oppress, torment   4 *manner*] nature   5 *wit*] good sense
6 *so*] i.e. that you love me   7 *testy*] irritable   11 *ill-wresting*] which
puts a bad sense on everything   13 *so*] i.e. believed; *belied*] slandered
14 *wide*] astray

141

In faith, I do not love thee with mine eyes,
For they in thee a thousand errors note;
But 'tis my heart that loves what they despise,
Who in despite of view is pleas'd to dote.
Nor are mine ears with thy tongue's tune delighted,
Nor tender feeling to base touches prone;
Nor taste nor smell desire to be invited
To any sensual feast with thee alone;
But my five wits nor my five senses can
Dissuade one foolish heart from serving thee,
Who leaves unsway'd the likeness of a man,
Thy proud heart's slave and vassal-wretch to be.
 Only my plague thus far I count my gain,
 That she that makes me sin awards me pain.

4 *view*] i.e. what the eyes see 6 *feeling*] sense of touch; *base*] gross, dishonouring 9 *But*] neither; *five wits*] mind in its five aspects (common wit, imagination, fantasy, estimation, memory) 11 Which, abandoning its sovereignty over me, leaves me only the appearance of being a man 13 *my plague*] what plagues me 14 *awards me pain*] makes me suffer for it

142

Love is my sin, and thy dear virtue hate,
Hate of my sin grounded on sinful loving.
O, but with mine compare thou thine own state,
And thou shalt find it merits not reproving;
Or if it do, not from those lips of thine,
That have profan'd their scarlet ornaments
And seal'd false bonds of love as oft as mine,
Robb'd others' beds' revenues of their rents.
Be it lawful I love thee as thou lov'st those
Whom thine eyes woo as mine importune thee!
Root pity in thy heart, that when it grows
Thy pity may deserve to pitied be.
        If thou dost seek to have what thou dost hide,
        By self example mayst thou be denied!

1   *thy dear virtue*] the virtue which you prize so highly   2   *sinful loving*]
(on your part)   4   *it*] i.e. my sin/love   8   Robbed other women of what is
due to them (sexually) and of what they would yield (i.e. children. *Revenues* is
stressed on the second syllable)   9   May it be lawful for me to . . .   13   *what
thou dost hide*] i.e. pity, which you do not show me   14   *self*] your own

143

Lo, as a careful housewife runs to catch
One of her feather'd creatures broke away,
Sets down her babe and makes all swift dispatch
In pursuit of the thing she would have stay,
Whilst her neglected child holds her in chase,
Cries to catch her whose busy care is bent
To follow that which flies before her face,
Not prizing her poor infant's discontent:
So runn'st thou after that which flies from thee,
Whilst I, thy babe, chase thee afar behind;
But if thou catch thy hope, turn back to me
And play the mother's part: kiss me, be kind.
So will I pray that thou mayst have thy Will
If thou turn back and my loud crying still.

1 *careful*] prudent, anxious; *housewife*] (pronounced 'hussif') 2 *feather'd creatures*] farmyard fowl (implicitly likened to 'your' befeathered gallants) 5 *holds her in chase*] chases her 6 *Cries*] weeps, shouts 8 *prizing*] paying attention to 11 *thy hope*] what you pursue 13 *Will*] (the same pun on the name as in 135 and 136)

144

Two loves I have, of comfort and despair,
Which like two spirits do suggest me still.
The better angel is a man right fair,
The worser spirit a woman colour'd ill.
To win me soon to hell my female evil
Tempteth my better angel from my side,
And would corrupt my saint to be a devil,
Wooing his purity with her foul pride.
And whether that my angel be turn'd fiend
Suspect I may, yet not directly tell;
But being both from me, both to each friend,
I guess one angel in another's hell.
      Yet this shall I ne'er know, but live in doubt
      Till my bad angel fire my good one out.

1 Two people are the object of my love, one bringing comfort, the other despair   2 *suggest*] prompt, tempt; *still*] continually   3 *right fair*] proper and handsome   4 *colour'd ill*] i.e. with dark hair and eyes   5 *To win me soon to hell*] i.e. to bring me to despair   8 *pride*] splendour of beauty, arrogance   10 *directly*] certainly   11 *from me*] away from me; *both to each friend*] each a friend of the other   12 *hell*] sexual parts   14 *fire . . . out*] drive away by passing on venereal disease

145

Those lips that love's own hand did make
Breath'd forth the sound that said 'I hate'
To me that languish'd for her sake;
But when she saw my woeful state,
Straight in her heart did mercy come,
Chiding that tongue that ever sweet
Was us'd in giving gentle doom,
And taught it thus anew to greet:
'I hate' she alter'd with an end
That follow'd it as gentle day
Doth follow night, who, like a fiend,
From heaven to hell is flown away.
        'I hate' from hate away she threw,
        And sav'd my life, saying 'not you.'

7 *us'd in giving*] accustomed to give; *doom*] judgement   8 *greet*] bring greeting

146

Poor soul, the centre of my sinful earth,
[. . .] these rebel powers that thee array;
Why dost thou pine within and suffer dearth,
Painting thy outward walls so costly gay?
Why so large cost, having so short a lease,
Dost thou upon thy fading mansion spend?
Shall worms, inheritors of this excess,
Eat up thy charge? Is this thy body's end?
Then, soul, live thou upon thy servant's loss,
And let that pine to aggravate thy store.
Buy terms divine in selling hours of dross;
Within be fed, without be rich no more.
 So shalt thou feed on Death, that feeds on men,
 And Death once dead, there's no more dying then.

---

1 *sinful earth*] i.e. body   2 (The printer of the 1609 Quarto repeated the last three words of line 1 by mistake at the start of this line; the two syllables that should fill the blank cannot be reconstructed, but something like 'thrall to' may be supposed); *powers*] (of the body); *array*] line up for battle, dress   3 *dearth*] famine, lack   8 *thy charge*] what you have spent so much on, your responsibility; *end*] fate, purpose   9 *thy servant's*] i.e. your body's   10 *aggravate*] increase; *store*] stock   11 *terms divine*] time in heaven   12 *without*] outside, in the body

147

My love is as a fever, longing still
For that which longer nurseth the disease,
Feeding on that which doth preserve the ill,
Th'uncertain sickly appetite to please.
My reason, the physician to my love,
Angry that his prescriptions are not kept,
Hath left me, and I desperate now approve
Desire is death, which physic did except.
Past cure I am, now reason is past care,
And frantic mad with evermore unrest.
My thoughts and my discourse as madmen's are,
At random from the truth, vainly express'd;
 For I have sworn thee fair, and thought thee bright,
 Who art as black as hell, as dark as night.

1 *still*] continually 3 *ill*] illness 6 *prescriptions . . . kept*] instructions
. . . followed 7 *approve*] learn that, display by my example that
8 *which . . . except*] (desire) which medicine forbade

148

O me, what eyes hath Love put in my head,
Which have no correspondence with true sight!
Or if they have, where is my judgement fled,
That censures falsely what they see aright?
If that be fair whereon my false eyes dote,
What means the world to say it is not so?
If it be not, then Love doth well denote
Love's eye is not so true as all men's 'no'.
How can it, O, how can Love's eye be true,
That is so vex'd with watching and with tears?
No marvel then, though I mistake my view:
The sun itself sees not till heaven clears.
     O cunning Love, with tears thou keep'st me blind,
     Lest eyes, well seeing, thy foul faults should find.

2   *no correspondence . . . sight*] no likeness to eyes that see true, nothing to do
with what is seen truly   4   *censures*] judges   7   *denote*] demonstrate
8   *as all men's 'no'*] as the eyes of all other men who see the object of my love
and reject it   10   *watching*] sleeplessness   11   It is no surprise, then, if I
do not see clearly, misunderstand what I see

149

Canst thou, O cruel, say I love thee not
When I against myself with thee partake?
Do I not think on thee when I forgot
Am of myself, all-tyrant, for thy sake?
Who hateth thee that I do call my friend?
On whom frown'st thou that I do fawn upon?
Nay, if thou lour'st on me, do I not spend
Revenge upon myself with present moan?
What merit do I in myself respect
That is so proud thy service to despise,
When all my best doth worship thy defect,
Commanded by the motion of thine eyes?
    But, love, hate on; for now I know thy mind:
    Those that can see thou lov'st, and I am blind.

2 *partake*] take sides   3–4 *forgot/ Am of*] am forgotten by   4 *all-tyrant*] (you who are a) tyrant in every respect   8 *present moan*] immediate lamentation, suffering   11 *defect*] imperfection

150

O, from what power hast thou this powerful might
With insufficiency my heart to sway,
To make me give the lie to my true sight
And swear that brightness doth not grace the day?
Whence hast thou this becoming of things ill,
That in the very refuse of thy deeds
There is such strength and warrantise of skill
That in my mind thy worst all best exceeds?
Who taught thee how to make me love thee more,
The more I hear and see just cause of hate?
O, though I love what others do abhor,
With others thou shouldst not abhor my state:
    If thy unworthiness rais'd love in me,
    More worthy I to be belov'd of thee.

2 *With insufficiency*] by means of weakness; *sway*] rule   3 *give . . . sight*] tell my eyes, which see true, that they lie   5 *becoming . . . ill*] power of making bad or ugly things look good   7 *warrantise of skill*] assurance of power to do

151

Love is too young to know what conscience is;
Yet who knows not conscience is born of love?
Then, gentle cheater, urge not my amiss,
Lest guilty of my faults thy sweet self prove.
For, thou betraying me, I do betray
My nobler part to my gross body's treason.
My soul doth tell my body that he may
Triumph in love; flesh stays no farther reason,
But rising at thy name doth point out thee
As his triumphant prize. Proud of this pride,
He is contented thy poor drudge to be,
To stand in thy affairs, fall by thy side.
> No want of conscience hold it that I call
> Her 'love' for whose dear love I rise and fall.

3 *urge not my amiss*] do not tax me with my fault   5 *betraying me*]
disclosing my fault, leading me into wrong, being unfaithful to me   8 *stays
... reason*] waits for no further argument   9 *rising*] i.e. in an erection (but
also 'rebelling')   10 *Proud ... pride*] Glorying in this state of erection,
sexually excited by this honour   12 *thy affairs*] (The sexual innuendo is
clear)

152

In loving thee thou know'st I am forsworn,
But thou art twice forsworn, to me love swearing:
In act thy bed-vow broke, and new faith torn
In vowing new hate after new love bearing.
But why of two oaths' breach do I accuse thee
When I break twenty? I am perjur'd most,
For all my vows are oaths but to misuse thee,
And all my honest faith in thee is lost.
For I have sworn deep oaths of thy deep kindness,
Oaths of thy love, thy truth, thy constancy;
And to enlighten thee gave eyes to blindness,
Or made them swear against the thing they see.
    For I have sworn thee fair – more perjur'd eye,
    To swear against the truth so foul a lie.

1 *am forsworn*] break my word (to the friend, to his wife)   3 *bed-vow*]
promise to share one bed (with one person)   7 *but*] whose upshot is merely;
misuse] treat badly, misrepresent   9 *of thy*] to the effect that you have
11 *enlighten thee*] make you shine; *gave ... blindness*] gave up my eyes to
blindness

153

Cupid laid by his brand and fell asleep.
A maid of Dian's this advantage found,
And his love-kindling fire did quickly steep
In a cold valley-fountain of that ground,
Which borrow'd from this holy fire of love
A dateless lively heat, still to endure,
And grew a seething bath which yet men prove
Against strange maladies a sovereign cure.
But at my mistress' eye Love's brand new fir'd,
The boy for trial needs would touch my breast;
I, sick withal, the help of bath desir'd,
And thither hied, a sad distemper'd guest,
  But found no cure; the bath for my help lies
  Where Cupid got new fire – my mistress' eyes.

1 *brand*] torch 2 *Dian's*] (Diana, goddess of chastity) 6 *dateless lively*] eternally living; *still*] forever 7 *seething*] boiling; *yet*] to this day; *prove*] find to be 10 *for trial*] to try it out 12 *hied*] hurried; *distemper'd*] sick, out of sorts

154

The little Love-god lying once asleep
Laid by his side his heart-inflaming brand,
Whilst many nymphs that vow'd chaste life to keep
Came tripping by; but in her maiden hand
The fairest votary took up that fire
Which many legions of true hearts had warm'd,
And so the general of hot desire
Was sleeping by a virgin hand disarm'd.
This brand she quenched in a cool well by,
Which from Love's fire took heat perpetual,
Growing a bath and healthful remedy
For men diseas'd; but I, my mistress' thrall,
    Came there for cure, and this by that I prove:
    Love's fire heats water, water cools not love.

1 *Love-god*] Cupid   2 *brand*] torch   5 *votary*] person who has
taken a vow (here, to chastity)   7 *general of hot desire*] i.e. Cupid, who
leads the forces of passion   9 *by*] nearby   11 *Growing*] becoming
12 *thrall*] slave

A LOVER'S COMPLAINT

From off a hill whose concave womb re-worded
A plaintful story from a sist'ring vale,
My spirits t'attend this double voice accorded,
And down I laid to list the sad-tun'd tale;
Ere long espied a fickle maid full pale,　　　　　　　5
Tearing of papers, breaking rings a-twain,
Storming her world with sorrow's wind and rain.

Upon her head a plaited hive of straw
Which fortified her visage from the sun,
Whereon the thought might think sometime it saw　　10
The carcass of a beauty spent and done.
Time had not scythed all that youth begun,
Nor youth all quit; but spite of heaven's fell rage,
Some beauty peep'd through lattice of sear'd age.

Oft did she heave her napkin to her eyne,　　　　　15
Which on it had conceited characters,
Laund'ring the silken figures in the brine
That season'd woe had pelleted in tears,
And often reading what contents it bears;
As often shrieking undistinguish'd woe　　　　　　20
In clamours of all size, both high and low.

3　*attend*] listen to; *accorded*] agreed　　　5　*fickle*] agitated, unstable
7　*Storming her world*] turning her world to storm　　　8　*plaited hive*] woven,
substantial hat　　9　*fortified*] protected　　10　*thought*] i.e. thinking person
13　*all quit*] left every part　　　14　*lattice*] (Perhaps suggested by the criss-
cross of *age*'s wrinkles)　　15　*heave*] raise; *napkin*] handkerchief; *eyne*] eyes
16　*conceited characters*] ingeniously meaningful inscriptions　　18　*season'd*]
long-lived, salted　　19　*what contents*] i.e. the *characters*　　20　*undistinguish'd*] inarticulate

Sometimes her levell'd eyes their carriage ride,
As they did batt'ry to the spheres intend;
Sometime diverted, their poor balls are tied
To th'orbed earth; sometimes they do extend 25
Their view right on, anon their gazes lend
To every place at once, and nowhere fix'd,
The mind and sight distractedly commix'd.

Her hair, nor loose nor tied in formal plait,
Proclaim'd in her a careless hand of pride; 30
For some, untuck'd, descended her sheav'd hat,
Hanging her pale and pined cheek beside,
Some in her threaden fillet still did bide,
And, true to bondage, would not break from thence,
Though slackly braided in loose negligence. 35

A thousand favours from a maund she drew
Of amber, crystal, and of bedded jet,
Which one by one she in a river threw
Upon whose weeping margin she was set,
Like usury, applying wet to wet, 40
Or monarch's hands that lets not bounty fall
Where want cries some, but where excess begs all.

---

22 *levell'd*] aimed (like a gun on its *carriage*)   23 *As*] as if; *spheres*]
heavens (thought to consist of a number of transparent spheres one within
another)   25 *orbed*] round   28 *distractedly commix'd*] wildly confused
30 *careless . . . pride*] indifferent to what she might take pride in   31 *sheav'd*]
woven of straw   33 *fillet*] hair-band   35 *slackly*] loosely   36 *favours*]
tokens of love; *maund*] basket   37 *bedded*] layered   39 *set*] sat
40 *Like usury*] (because usury adds money to money by accumulating interest
into capital)   42 *cries*] asks for

Of folded schedules had she many a one
Which she perus'd, sigh'd, tore, and gave the flood;
Crack'd many a ring of posied gold and bone,   45
Bidding them find their sepulchres in mud;
Found yet more letters sadly penn'd in blood,
With sleided silk feat and affectedly
Enswath'd, and seal'd to curious secrecy.

These often bath'd she in her fluxive eyes,   50
And often kiss'd, and often 'gan to tear;
Cried 'O false blood, thou register of lies,
What unapproved witness dost thou bear!
Ink would have seem'd more black and damned here!'
This said, in top of rage the lines she rents,   55
Big discontent so breaking their contents.

A reverend man that graz'd his cattle nigh,
Sometime a blusterer that the ruffle knew
Of court, of city, and had let go by
The swiftest hours observed as they flew,   60
Towards this afflicted fancy fastly drew,
And, privileg'd by age, desires to know
In brief the grounds and motives of her woe.

---

43 *schedules*] papers   45 *posied*] bearing mottoes   48 *sleided*] separated into threads; *feat*] neatly; *affectedly*] lovingly   49 *to curious secrecy*]
cleverly to make secret   50 *fluxive*] flowing   53 *unapproved*]
false, proved not true   55 *top*] height; *rents*] tears   57 *reverend*]
(presumably because old)   58 *ruffle*] noise and bustle   61 *afflicted*
fancy] person afflicted by love; *fastly*] close by

So slides he down upon his grained bat,
And comely distant sits he by her side, 65
When he again desires her, being sat,
Her grievance with his hearing to divide;
If that from him there may be aught applied
Which may her suffering ecstasy assuage,
'Tis promis'd in the charity of age. 70

'Father,' she says, 'though in me you behold
The injury of many a blasting hour,
Let it not tell your judgement I am old;
Not age, but sorrow over me hath power.
I might as yet have been a spreading flower, 75
Fresh to myself, if I had self-applied
Love to myself, and to no love beside.

'But, woe is me, too early I attended
A youthful suit – it was to gain my grace –
O, one by Nature's outwards so commended 80
That maidens' eyes stuck over all his face.
Love lack'd a dwelling and made him her place,
And when in his fair parts she did abide
She was new lodg'd and newly deified.

64 *slides . . . bat*] he passes easily down upon his wooden staff   65 *comely distant*] at a decent distance   67 *divide*] share   69 *suffering ecstasy*] violent fit of pain   72 *blasting*] blighting   76 *Fresh to myself*] unblasted in my own eyes   78 *attended*] listened to   79 *grace*] favour   80 *Nature's outwards*] the appearance given him by Nature

'His browny locks did hang in crooked curls,   85
And every light occasion of the wind
Upon his lips their silken parcels hurls.
What's sweet to do, to do will aptly find;
Each eye that saw him did enchant the mind,
For on his visage was in little drawn   90
What largeness thinks in paradise was sawn.

'Small show of man was yet upon his chin;
His phoenix down began but to appear,
Like unshorn velvet, on that termless skin
Whose bare outbragg'd the web it seem'd to wear,   95
Yet show'd his visage by that cost more dear,
And nice affections wavering stood in doubt
If best were as it was, or best without.

'His qualities were beauteous as his form,
For maiden-tongu'd he was, and thereof free.   100
Yet if men mov'd him, was he such a storm
As oft twixt May and April is to see
When winds breathe sweet, unruly though they be.
His rudeness so with his authoriz'd youth
Did livery falseness in a pride of truth.   105

86 *light occasion*] gentle stirring   87 *parcels*] bundles   88 *What's* . . .
find] What is pleasant to do will readily find people to do it   91 *What
. . . sawn*] What is thought to have been seen (or sown?) full-scale in Eden
93 *phoenix*] unparalleled (there was only one phoenix)   94 *termless*]
indescribable   95 *Whose . . . wear*] whose unadorned skin spoke more
bravely than the nascent beard it hardly seemed to be clothed in (*web* = cloth)
96 *cost*] expenditure, growth (of beard); *dear*] highly valued, loved   97 *nice
affections*] those discriminating in what drew them to him   100 *maiden-
tongu'd*] pure in speech, soft-spoken   104–5] His roughness to such an
extent licensed by his youth dressed deceitfulness in proud claims to truthfulness

'Well could he ride, and often men would say
"That horse his mettle from his rider takes;
Proud of subjection, noble by the sway,
What rounds, what bounds, what course, what stop he
    makes!"
And controversy hence a question takes,   110
Whether the horse by him became his deed,
Or he his manage by th'well-doing steed.

'But quickly on this side the verdict went:
His real habitude gave life and grace
To appertainings and to ornament,   115
Accomplish'd in himself, not in his case.
All aids, themselves made fairer by their place,
Came for additions; yet their purpos'd trim
Piec'd not his grace, but were all grac'd by him.

'So on the tip of his subduing tongue   120
All kind of arguments and question deep,
All replication prompt and reason strong,
For his advantage still did wake and sleep.
To make the weeper laugh, the laugher weep,
He had the dialect and different skill,   125
Catching all passions in his craft of will,

108 *noble by the sway*] made noble by the power to which he submits
109 *rounds . . . bounds . . . course . . . stop*] equestrian manoeuvres
111–12 Whether the horse performed well thanks to its rider, or the rider
thanks to the horse   114 *real habitude*] essential nature   116 *case*]
outward circumstance   117 *by their place*] by being applied to him
118 *Came for additions*] offered themselves as supplementary graces; *purpos'd
trim*] intended ornament   119 *Piec'd*] increased   120 *subduing*] con-
quering   122 *replication prompt*] ready reply   125 *dialect and different skill*] skill of varying his language to suit the occasion   126 *craft of
will*] persuasive art

'That he did in the general bosom reign
Of young, of old, and sexes both enchanted,
To dwell with him in thoughts, or to remain
In personal duty, following where he haunted.   130
Consents bewitch'd, ere he desire, have granted,
And dialogu'd for him what he would say,
Ask'd their own wills, and made their wills obey.

'Many there were that did his picture get
To serve their eyes, and in it put their mind,   135
Like fools that in th'imagination set
The goodly objects which abroad they find
Of lands and mansions, theirs in thought assign'd,
And labour in more pleasures to bestow them
Than the true gouty landlord which doth owe them.   140

'So many have, that never touch'd his hand,
Sweetly suppos'd them mistress of his heart.
My woeful self, that did in freedom stand,
And was my own fee-simple, not in part,
What with his art in youth, and youth in art,   145
Threw my affections in his charmed power,
Reserv'd the stalk and gave him all my flower.

127 *That*] so that   130 *where he haunted*] in his haunts   131 *Consents bewitch'd*] people charmed into consenting   137 *objects*] images; *abroad*] in the world   139 And finding more pleasure in the work of administering them   140 *owe*] own   144 *was my own fee-simple*] had full possession of myself (like freehold property)

'Yet did I not, as some my equals did,
Demand of him, nor being desired yielded.
Finding myself in honour so forbid,   150
With safest distance I mine honour shielded.
Experience for me many bulwarks builded
Of proofs new bleeding, which remain'd the foil
Of this false jewel and his amorous spoil.

'But ah, who ever shunn'd by precedent   155
The destin'd ill she must herself assay,
Or forc'd examples 'gainst her own content
To put the by-past perils in her way?
Counsel may stop a while what will not stay;
For when we rage, advice is often seen,   160
By blunting us, to make our wills more keen.

'Nor gives it satisfaction to our blood
That we must curb it upon others' proof,
To be forbod the sweets that seems so good
For fear of harms that preach in our behoof.   165
O appetite, from judgement stand aloof!
The one a palate hath that needs will taste,
Though Reason weep, and cry it is thy last.

---

153 *proofs new bleeding*] evidences still fresh of injury; *foil*] dark background to show off a jewel   155 *by precedent*] thanks to previous example
156 *assay*] make trial of   157 *forc'd*] urged; *content*] i.e. supposed
happiness   158 *by-past perils*] dangers suffered in the past   159 *Counsel*]
advice; *stay*] i.e. stay for ever   161 *blunting us*] taking the edge off our
desires   162 *blood*] passions   163 *proof*] experience   164 *forbod*]
forbidden   165 *harms*] i.e. *proofs new bleeding*; *behoof*] behalf

'For further I could say this man's untrue,
And knew the patterns of his foul beguiling,   170
Heard where his plants in others' orchards grew,
Saw how deceits were gilded in his smiling,
Knew vows were ever brokers to defiling,
Thought characters and words merely but art,
And bastards of his foul adulterate heart.   175

'And long upon these terms I held my city
Till thus he gan besiege me: "Gentle maid,
Have of my suffering youth some feeling pity,
And be not of my holy vows afraid.
That's to ye sworn to none was ever said;   180
For feasts of love I have been call'd unto,
Till now did ne'er invite nor never woo.

'"All my offences that abroad you see
Are errors of the blood, none of the mind.
Love made them not; with acture they may be,   185
Where neither party is nor true nor kind.
They sought their shame that so their shame did find,
And so much less of shame in me remains
By how much of me their reproach contains.

169   For I could say more of this man's lack of truth and honour
170   *patterns*] examples (of those he had beguiled), methods (of his beguiling)
173   *brokers to*] agents for   174   *characters*] written language (as opposed
to spoken *words*)   175   *adulterate*] impure, adulterous   176   *city*]
stronghold   183   *abroad*] in the world   185   *with acture they may be*]
i.e. they may come about (the word *acture* is only found here; the effect is
generally evasive)   189   As much of my fault may be blamed upon them

'"Among the many that mine eyes have seen,   190
Not one whose flame my heart so much as warm'd
Or my affection put to th' smallest teen,
Or any of my leisures ever charm'd.
Harm have I done to them, but ne'er was harm'd,
Kept hearts in liveries, but mine own was free,   195
And reign'd commanding in his monarchy.

'"Look here what tributes wounded fancies sent me
Of pallid pearls and rubies red as blood,
Figuring that they their passions likewise lent me
Of grief and blushes, aptly understood   200
In bloodless white and the encrimson'd mood –
Effects of terror and dear modesty
Encamp'd in hearts, but fighting outwardly.

'"And lo, behold, these talents of their hair,
With twisted metal amorously empleach'd,   205
I have receiv'd from many a several fair,
Their kind acceptance weepingly beseech'd,
With th'annexions of fair gems enrich'd,
And deep-brain'd sonnets that did amplify
Each stone's dear nature, worth, and quality.   210

192   *teen*] trouble   193   *leisures*] moments of leisure   195   *in liveries*] i.e.
as servants   197   *wounded fancies*] sick and doting women   199   *Figuring*]
expressing symbolically   203   *but fighting outwardly*] only apparently resist-
ing   204   *talents*] riches   205   *amorously*] lovingly; *empleach'd*] inwoven
206   *many a several fair*] many a beautiful woman   208   *annexions*]
addition   209   *amplify*] enlarge on

'"The diamond? – why, 'twas beautiful and hard,
Whereto his invis'd properties did tend;
The deep-green em'rald, in whose fresh regard
Weak sights their sickly radiance do amend,
The heaven-hued sapphire and the opal blend   215
With objects manifold – each several stone,
With wit well blazon'd, smil'd or made some moan.

'"Lo, all these trophies of affections hot,
Of pensiv'd and subdued desires the tender,
Nature hath charg'd me that I hoard them not,   220
But yield them up where I myself must render –
That is, to you, my origin and ender;
For these of force must your oblations be,
Since, I their altar, you enpatron me.

'"O then advance of yours that phraseless hand   225
Whose white weighs down the airy scale of praise;
Take all these similes to your own command,
Hallow'd with sighs that burning lungs did raise.
What me, your minister, for you obeys,
Works under you, and to your audit comes   230
Their distract parcels in combined sums.

212 (1) As a result of its unseen properties, (2) ?to which the desired and
detested qualities of the young man were parallel. (*Invis'd* occurs nowhere else)
213 *in whose fresh regard*] in whose invigorating light   214 *radiance*] (It
was thought that eyes saw by sending out rays)   215–16 *blend/ With
objects manifold*] compounded of many colours and forms   217 *blazon'd*]
expounded   218 *affections hot*] passionate desires   219 *pensiv'd*]
saddened; *tender*] offering   220 *charg'd*] commanded   221 *myself
must render*] must make payment of myself   222 *ender*] person who will
end my life   223 *oblations*] offerings   224 *you enpatron me*] you are
the patron saint to whom I am dedicated   225 *phraseless*] indescribably
beautiful   226 Whose whiteness is too much to be adequately praised (and
makes praise seem slight by comparison)   229 *minister*] agent   230 *to
your audit*] to account to you   231 *distract parcels*] separate lots

' "Lo, this device was sent me from a nun,
A sister sanctified of holiest note,
Which late her noble suit in court did shun,
Whose rarest havings made the blossoms dote;   235
For she was sought by spirits of richest coat,
But kept cold distance, and did thence remove
To spend her living in eternal love.

' "But O, my sweet, what labour is't to leave
The thing we have not, mast'ring what not strives,   240
Planing the place which did no form receive,
Playing patient sports in unconstrained gyves!
She that her fame so to herself contrives
The scars of battle scapeth by the flight,
And makes her absence valiant, not her might.   245

' "O, pardon me, in that my boast is true!
The accident which brought me to her eye
Upon the moment did her force subdue,
And now she would the caged cloister fly.
Religious love put out religion's eye.   250
Not to be tempted would she be immur'd,
And now to tempt all liberty procur'd.

232 *device*] emblematic trinket   234 *late*] recently; *suit*] business
235 *havings*] endowments; *blossoms*] young courtiers (ornaments of the court)
236 *richest coat*] highest breeding   238 *living*] life; *eternal*] (because religious)   240 *what not strives*] something that does not resist   241–2 Making
smooth the place (e.g. on a jewel) which had received no impression, enduring
patiently the restraint of fetters that do not restrain   243 *fame*] reputation
245 And is considered valiant on the basis of absence from the battle rather
than from contest in it   250 *Religious love*] (secular) love made into a
religion   251 *immur'd*] put behind the walls (of a convent)   252 (*all* is
either the object of *tempt* or qualifies *liberty*)

'"How mighty then you are, O hear me tell!
The broken bosoms that to me belong
Have emptied all their fountains in my well,   255
And mine I pour your ocean all among.
I strong o'er them, and you o'er me being strong,
Must for your victory us all congest,
As compound love to physic your cold breast.

'"My parts had power to charm a sacred nun,   260
Who, disciplin'd, ay, dieted in grace,
Believ'd her eyes when they t'assail begun,
All vows and consecrations giving place.
O most potential love: vow, bond, nor space
In thee hath neither sting, knot, nor confine,   265
For thou art all, and all things else are thine.

'"When thou impressest, what are precepts worth
Of stale example? When thou wilt inflame,
How coldly those impediments stand forth
Of wealth, of filial fear, law, kindred, fame.   270
Love's arms are peace, 'gainst rule, 'gainst sense, 'gainst
     shame;
And sweetens in the suff'ring pangs it bears
The aloes of all forces, shocks, and fears.

254 *bosoms*] i.e. hearts   255 *well*] stream   258 *for*] in consequence
of; *congest*] bring together   259 *compound*] composite, like a *compound*
drug   260 *parts*] qualities   261 *dieted*] regulated   262 *t'assail*] i.e.
to assail her heart   264 *potential*] powerful; *space*] i.e. limitation of space
265 *confine*] limitation   267 *impressest*] conscript   270 *fame*] reputation   271 *are peace*] i.e conquer; *rule . . . sense . . . shame*] (all conquered
by love)   272 *sweetens*] (love) makes sweet; *bears*] endures   273 *aloes*]
i.e. bitterness (*aloes* being a bitter herb)

'"Now all these hearts that do on mine depend,
Feeling it break, with bleeding groans they pine,　　275
And, supplicant, their sighs to you extend
To leave the batt'ry that you make 'gainst mine,
Lending soft audience to my sweet design,
And credent soul to that strong-bonded oath
That shall prefer and undertake my troth."　　280

'This said, his wat'ry eyes he did dismount,
Whose sights till then were levell'd on my face.
Each cheek a river running from a fount
With brinish current downward flow'd apace.
O, how the channel to the stream gave grace,　　285
Who glaz'd with crystal gate the glowing roses
That flame through water which their hue encloses.

'O father, what a hell of witchcraft lies
In the small orb of one particular tear!
But with the inundation of the eyes　　290
What rocky heart to water will not wear?
What breast so cold that is not warmed here?
O cleft effect! Cold modesty, hot wrath,
Both fire from hence and chill extincture hath.

275 *bleeding groans*] (Sighs were believed to consume blood)　　279 *credent*]
trustful, believing　　280 *prefer and undertake*] advance and see through
281 *wat'ry*] tearful; *dismount*] turn away (imagery from artillery)　　282 *levell'd*]
fixed　　286 Which (the stream) glazed the glowing roses (of his cheeks) with
its crystal barrier　　289 *particular*] single　　294 *hence*] the *inundation*
of the eyes; *extincture*] extinction

'For lo, his passion, but an art of craft, 295
Even there resolv'd my reason into tears.
There my white stole of chastity I daff'd,
Shook off my sober guards and civil fears;
Appear to him as he to me appears,
All melting, though our drops this diff'rence bore: 300
His poison'd me, and mine did him restore.

'In him a plenitude of subtle matter,
Applied to cautels, all strange forms receives,
Of burning blushes or of weeping water,
Or sounding paleness; and he takes and leaves, 305
In either's aptness, as it best deceives –
To blush at speeches rank, to weep at woes,
Or to turn white and sound at tragic shows;

'That not a heart which in his level came
Could 'scape the hail of his all-hurting aim, 310
Showing fair nature is both kind and tame,
And, veil'd in them, did win whom he would maim.
Against the thing he sought he would exclaim;
When he most burn'd in heart-wish'd luxury,
He preach'd pure maid and prais'd cold chastity. 315

---

295 *art of craft*] artifice of cunning   296 *resolv'd*] transformed
297 *daff'd*] put off   298 *guards*] defences; *civil*] decorous, grave
300 *drops*] tears   302 *subtle matter*] fine-spun ideas, cunning   303 *cautels*]
deceits   305 *sounding*] swooning   307 *rank*] coarse   308 *sound*]
swoon   309 *level*] range   310 *hail*] shower, volley   311 *Showing*]
which showed, which appeared to show; *tame*] i.e. not savage   312 *them*]
i.e. the *blushes* etc. of the previous stanza   314 *luxury*] lust

'Thus merely with the garment of a grace
The naked and concealed fiend he cover'd,
That th'unexperient gave the tempter place,
Which like a cherubin above them hover'd.
Who, young and simple, would not be so lover'd?   320
Ay me, I fell, and yet do question make
What I should do again for such a sake.

'O, that infected moisture of his eye,
O, that false fire which in his cheek so glow'd,
O, that forc'd thunder from his heart did fly,   325
O, that sad breath his spongy lungs bestow'd,
O, all that borrow'd motion, seeming ow'd,
Would yet again betray the fore-betray'd,
And new pervert a reconciled maid.'

317 *concealed*] hidden (once *cover'd*)   318 *unexperient*] unexperienced;
gave ... place] granted entry, audience   323 *infected*] diseased, corrupt
325 *forc'd*] unnatural, artificial   327 *ow'd*] owned, his own   328 *fore-
betray'd*] already once betrayed   329 *reconciled*] repentant, calmed,
acquiescent

SHAKESPEARE AND HIS CRITICS

Serious criticism of Shakespeare's sonnets does not begin until the twentieth century. We know little of their reception in Shakespeare's own time. Francis Meres, in *Palladis Tamia, Wits Treasury* (1598) writes of 'Shakespeare ... his sugred Sonnets among his private friends' and characterizes him as one of 'the most passionate among us to bewaile and bemoane the perplexities of Love', but this does not tell us much more than that some poems were circulating in 1598 and that the author was admired. A few sonnets do survive in manuscript collections from the early seventeenth century but their number does not suggest great popularity, and critical comment is almost nonexistent until near the end of the eighteenth century, when Edmond Malone produced the first scholarly edition of the poems, with notes by another editor, George Steevens. The two were at odds about the sonnets. Steevens, for example, took exception to Sonnet 20: 'It is impossible to read this fulsome panegyrick, addressed to a male object, without an equal mixture of disgust and indignation' and complained at the 'laboured perplexities of language, and ... studied deformities of style' to be found in the sonnets as a whole. Malone replied:

> When they are described as a mass of affectation, pedantry, circumlocution, and nonsense, the picture appears to me overcharged. Their great defects seem to be a want of variety, and the majority of them not being directed to a female, to whom alone such ardent expressions of esteem could with propriety be addressed.

In his edition of 1790, Malone returned to Shakespeare's defence, observing that 'such addresses to men, however indelicate, were customary in our author's time, and neither imparted criminality, nor were esteemed indecorous'.

The two issues of obscure and affected style and the 'indelicacy' of the sonnets' being addressed to a man recur in the remarks of Wordsworth and Coleridge, annotations to the poems in a volume of Anderson's *British Poets*, one of a number of similar collections published in the late eighteenth century. These annotations were made some time between 1800 and 1803. Wordsworth objected to the sonnets to the Dark Lady (127 onwards) as 'worse than a puzzle-peg ... abominably harsh obscure & worthless'.

> The others are for the most part much better, have many fine lines very fine lines and passages. They are also in many places warm with passion. Their chief faults, and heavy ones, are sameness, tediousness, quaintness, & elaborate obscurity.

Wordsworth thought Sonnet 116 ('Let me not to the marriage of true minds') to be the best. Coleridge was far more enthusiastic:

> I see no elaborate obscurity & very little quaintness – nor do I know any Sonnets that will bear such frequent perusal: so rich in metre, so full of Thought & *exquisitest* Diction.

He interpreted Shakespeare's relation to the young man in the light of 'the Chapter in Potter's Antiquities on the Greek lovers':

> This pure Love Shakespeare appears to have felt – to have been no way ashamed of it – or even to have suspected that others could have suspected it / yet at the same time he knew that so strong a Love would have been made more compleatly a Thing of Permanence & Reality, & have been blessed more by Nature & taken under her most especial protection if this Object of his Love had been at the same Time a possible Object of Desire ...

In his *Table Talk* for 13 May 1833 he further expands upon this 'affection beyond Friendship and wholly aloof from Appetite' in relation to the sonnets whilst at the same time asserting that they

> could only have come from a man deeply in love, and in love with a woman – and there is one Sonnet [presumably Sonnet 20], which from its incongruity of tone I take to be a purposed blind.

On this occasion, he found the sonnets to be characterized by 'boundless fertility, and labored condensation of thought, with perfection of sweetness in rhythm and metre ... the essentials in the budding of a great poet'.

Coleridge is eloquent, but the issue of homosexuality evidently niggles and takes a deal of talking round. Keats's remark in a letter to J. H. Reynolds of 22 November 1817 is briefer, simpler, more affecting and more provocative of thought: 'I ne'er found so many beauties in the Sonnets – they seem to be full of fine things said unintentionally in the intensity of working out conceits ... He has left nothing to say about nothing or anything ...'

It is not until we get to Tennyson that we find anything like enthusiasm again. Hazlitt was on the whole unenchanted by the sonnets, and Landor, in his third series of *Imaginary Conversations* (1828), comes out with a marvellous image of ambiguous appreciation:

> They are hot and pothery: there is much condensation, little delicacy; like raspberry jam without cream, without crust, without bread, to break its viscidity. But I would rather sit down to one of them again, than to a string of such musty sausages as are exposed in our streets at the present dull season.

Tennyson's way of putting things is less literary than this, but a lot more positive, despite the curious formation of his sentence which gives with one hand and takes away with the other. Edward Fitzgerald, poet of the *Rubaiyat*, includes among his notes of conversations with Tennyson that took place round about 1835 – the notes themselves date from fifteen years or so later – the following remark:

> Sometimes I think Shakespeare's Sonnets finer than his Plays – which is of course absurd. For it is knowledge of the Plays that makes the Sonnets so fine.

However phrased, this makes it clear that he did think the sonnets fine. It was a sentiment he shared with his great friend Arthur Hallam, and the shadow of the sonnets hangs over the whole of Tennyson's own long series of elegies for the dead Hallam, *In Memoriam* (1850). Hallam's father Henry, sensitive to the imputation of homosexuality and of his son's admiration and that of his friend, thought it 'impossible not to wish that Shakespeare had never written' the sonnets (in his *Introduction to the Literature of Europe*, 1839). Tennyson in later life contradicted him: 'Henry Hallam made a great mistake about them: they are noble.'

In the mid-nineteenth century the sonnets became the focus

for much biographical speculation, of which an illuminating and entertaining account is given in S. Schoenbaum, *Shakespeare's Lives* (1970). Oscar Wilde's extravaganza 'The Portrait of Mr W. H.' identifying, in the ambiguous form of a story, 'Mr W. H.' with an imaginary boy-actor Willie Hughes, is the offspring of such speculations adapted to allow of Wilde's own fantasies about girlish boys. It is a teasing work in more senses than one which may be most significant to us in its willingness to consider *A Lover's Complaint* as of a piece with the sonnets. The opposite tack to such biographical interpretation is taken by those scholars who, like Sir Sidney Lee, dealt in the wide range of other sonnets that Shakespeare might have modelled his own upon – sonnets by Tasso, Du Bellay, Ronsard or Desportes as well as the author's fellow-countrymen Constable, Daniel, Drayton and Watson. The tendency of such work was to downplay the biographical by emphasizing the conventional: 'the autobiographical element, although it may not be dismissed altogether, is seen to shrink to slender proportions' observed Sir Sidney with a touch of self-congratulation in the second edition of *A Life of William Shakespeare* (1916).

If criticism is writing that articulates for us the kind of pleasure that a work of literature gives and the value which it is legitimate to set by it, then there is a little, but not much, in the remarks so far recorded that is criticism. To articulate what something does for us does not necessarily involve close analysis of the kind that practical criticism has made familiar. A deep intuitive understanding may after all produce the flash of words that does the job, and perhaps that is true of remarks by Coleridge and Keats here. But where so much seems difficult to seize and obscure – and that is certainly the case with the relationship of poet and young man – there is a great deal to be said for getting close to the poems and looking at them in detail. The first critics to do this – critics, rather than editors – were Laura Riding and Robert Graves, in *A Survey of Modernist Poetry* (1927).

This was not perhaps the place in which you would expect to find writing on the sonnets, but Riding and Graves wanted to justify the apparent typographical perversity of the modern poet E. E. Cummings by showing that Shakespeare's meaning was equally and similarly dependent on effects of punctuation that had little to do with the conventional. They contrasted a modernized text of Sonnet 129 with the version found in Shakespeare's *Sonnets* (1609) to the advantage of the latter. Thus they note that 1609 'Had, hauing, and in quest, to haue extreame,' becomes in the modern version 'Had, having, and in quest to have, extreme;' – they comment:

> The comma between *in quest* and *to haue extreame* has been moved forward to separate *haue* from *extreame*. This line originally stood for a number of interwoven meanings:
>
> 1. The taker of the bait, the man in pursuit and in possession of lust, is made mad: is so made that he experiences both extremes at once. (What these extremes are the lines following show.)
>
> 2. The *Had, hauing and in quest*, might well have been written in parentheses. They explain, by way of interjection, that lust comprises all the stages of lust: the after-lust period (*Had*), the actual experience of lust (*hauing*), and the anticipation of lust (*in quest*); and that the extremes of lust are felt in all these stages (*to haue extreame* – ie to have in extreme degree).
>
> 3. Further, one stage in lust is like the others, is as extreme as the others. All the distinctions made in the poem between *lust in action* and *till action lust*, between lust *In pursut* and lust *in possession* are made to show that in the end there are no real distinctions. *Had, hauing and in quest* is the summing up of this fact.
>
> 4. *Had* and *hauing* double the sense of *possession* to match the double sense of *action* implied by *Th'expence of Spirit in a waste of shame*; and *in quest* naturally refers to *In pursut*, which in turn recalls *till action*.
>
> 5. Throughout the poem it must be kept in mind that words qualifying the lust-interest refer interchangeably to the man who lusts, the object of lust and lust in the abstract. This interchangeability accounts for the apparently ungrammatical effect of the line.

With the emended punctuation the line has only one narrow sense, and this not precisely Shakespeare's; the semicolon placed after *so* of the preceding line, cuts the close co-operation between them. The shifting of the comma not only removes a pause where Shakespeare put one, and thus changes the rhythm, but the line itself loses point and does not pull its weight. In this punctuation the *whole* line ought to be put into parenthesis, as being a mere repetition. The *to haue* linked with *in quest* is superfluous; *extreme* set off by itself is merely a descriptive adjective already used. Moreover, when the line is thus isolated between two semicolons,

Had, hauing, etc., instead of effecting a harmony between the interchangeable senses, disjoints them and becomes ungrammatical. *Mad in pursuit, and in possession so* refers only to *the taker mad.* The next line, *A blisse in proofe and proud and very wo,* should explain *to have extreame*; it is not merely another parenthetical line as in the emended version. To fulfil the paradox implied in *extreame* it should mean that lust is a bliss during the proof and after the proof, and also *very wo* (truly woe) during and after the proof. The emended line, *A bliss in proof, and proved, a very woe,* which refers only to lust in the abstract, not equally to the man who lusts, means that lust is a bliss during the proof but a woe after the proof – and thus denies what Shakespeare has been at pains to show all along, that lust is all things at all times.

Once the editors began repunctuating the line they had to tamper with the words themselves. A comma after *proof* demanded a comma after *proud.* A comma after *proud* made it necessary to change *and very wo* so that it should apply to *proud* only. Another semicolon which they have put at the end of this line again breaks the continuity of the sense: the succeeding line becomes only another antithesis or rhetorical balance ('a joy in prospect, but a dream in retrospect,' to repeat the sense of 'a bliss during proof but woe after proof'), instead of carrying on the intricate and careful argument that runs without a stop through the whole sestet. The importance of the line is that it takes all the meanings in the poem one stage further. Lust in the extreme goes beyond both bliss and woe: it goes beyond reality. It is no longer lust *Had, hauing and in quest*; it is lust face to face with *love.* Even when consummated, lust still stands before an unconsummated joy, a proposed joy, and proposed not as a joy possible of consummation but as one only to be known through the dream by which lust leads itself on, the dream behind which this proposed joy, this love, seems to lie. This is the over-riding meaning of the line. It has other meanings, but they all defer to this. For example, it may also be read: 'Before a joy can be proposed, it must first be renounced as a real joy, it must be put behind as a dream'; or: 'Before the man in lust is a prospect of joy, yet he knows by experience that this is only a dream'; or: 'Beforehand he says that he proposed lust to be a joy, afterwards he says that it came as involuntarily as a dream'; or: 'Before (in face of) a joy proposed only as a consequence of a dream, with a dream impelling him from behind.' All these and even more readings of the line are possible and legitimate, and each reading could in turn be made to explain precisely why the taker is made mad, or how lust is *to haue extreame*, or why it is both *a blisse* and *very wo*.

The implicit message here is that the poem gives pleasure *because* it is difficult, because it finely articulates what is difficult to grasp, the relationship between lust and love. 'Making poetry easy for the reader should mean showing clearly how difficult it really is', say the two critics (who were themselves both good poets of rather different kinds).

Graves and Riding were the first to expound in any detail the wealth of meanings and nuance that the sonnets contain, and it is helpful to be aware of their views when reading a modernized text such as that provided here. Modernization undoubtedly makes things easier by simplifying. But there is a case for modernization nevertheless – that it provides a starting point and may even nudge in the right direction, whilst an old-spelling text may baffle and disturb without rendering any more accurately than its rival what the author originally wrote. (Punctuation may be the printer's not the author's.)

A Survey of Modernist Poetry famously gave birth to one of the great books of twentieth-century criticism, William Empson's *Seven Types of Ambiguity* (1930), which contains several acute analyses of the sonnets very much in the Graves-Riding manner. When they describe Shakespeare as writing not 'in the syntax of prose but in a sensitive poetic flow' he writes of 'an interpenetrating and, as it were, fluid writing in the sonnets in which phrases will go either with the sentence before or after, and there is no break in the movement of the thought'. This emphasis on unity is an implied riposte to the remark by T. S. Eliot in his 1919 essay 'Hamlet': '*Hamlet, like the sonnets* [my italics], is full of some stuff that the writer could not drag to light, contemplate or manipulate into art.' Empson is concerned not only to show that the sonnets are 'full of ... stuff' (in the essay on Sonnet 94 in his *Some Versions of Pastoral* (1935) he computes '4096 movements of thought' in the poem, 'with other possibilities') but that they do hang together, though not in a way easy to define; he ends his discussion of Sonnet 73 in *Seven Types* as follows:

A literary conundrum is tedious, and these meanings are only worth detaching in so far as they are dissolved into the single mood of the poem. Many people would say that they cannot all be dissolved, and an evidently delicate and slender Sonnet ought not to take so much explaining, whatever its wealth of reference and feeling, that Shakespeare, if all this is true, wrote without properly clarifying his mind. One might protest *via* the epithet 'natural', which has stuck to Shakespeare through so many literary fashions; that he had a wide rather than a sharp focus to his mind; that he snatched ideas almost at random from its balanced but multitudinous activity; that this is likely to be more so rather than less in his personal poetry; and that in short (as Macaulay said in a very different connection) the reader must take such grammar as he can get and be thankful. One might apologise by saying that people have always read obscure meanings into Shakespeare, secure in the feeling, 'If it means less, why is it so beautiful?' and that this analysis can only be offered as another mode of approaching so mysterious a totality, another glance at the effects of language. Or it may boldly be said that the composition of feeling, which never falls apart among these ambiguities (it [Sonnet 83] is, on any interpretation, pained, bitter, tender and admiring; Shakespeare is being abandoned by W. H., and stiffly apologising for not having been servile to him), rises and is clinched plainly in the final couplet; we are reminded of the references to the roving eye glancing round for new conquests; Shakespeare includes the whole ambiguity in his enthusiasm; the worth and sin, the beauty and painting, are all delightful to him, and too subtle to be grasped.

From this point on the tide turns decisively in favour of the sonnets' excellence. John Crowe Ransom in his essay of 1938 'Shakespeare at Sonnets' is one of the few to advance damaging criticisms of the sonnets, and his objections are based on structure:

Probably Shakespeare's usual structural difficulty consists about equally in having to pad out his quatrains, if three good co-ordinates do not offer themselves, and in having to squeeze the couplet too flat, or else extend its argument upward into the proper territory of the quatrains. But when both these things happen at once, the obvious remark is that the poet should have reverted to the Italian sonnet.

(*The World's Body*, 1938)

Crowe Ransom, in other words, thought that Shakespeare did not sufficiently respect the division of his sonnet into 3 units of 4 lines each followed by one of 2 (4–4–4–2) and felt that the Italian form which simply contrasts a longer and a shorter section (8–6) would have suited the poet's book better. Admirers of Shakespeare's 'fluid unit' might argue that the more the poet transgressed the formal boundaries he had established for himself, the more chance he had to achieve a unity transcending that conventionally implied by his chosen form: precisely, a *fluid* unity, blurring the categories of rational expectation.

This is not quite the line that has been taken by academic critics of the sonnets who have, instead, emphasized other aspects of form than those implied by rhyme-schemes. Indeed, M. M. Mahood, in her book *Shakespeare's Wordplay* (1957) argues that the poet uses 'a subdued sort of wordplay' as a means of evening up the extreme contrast between the couplet and the preceding twelve lines: 'It allows him to introduce the counter-movement of thought before the reader is aware of its presence, so that the final couplet satisfies both by conscious surprise and by its fulfilment of a subconscious expectation.' An example is certainly in order, and I choose her discussion of Sonnet 30. Since she, like many recent critics, quotes in old spelling, and since modernization is an issue of which the reader is by now aware, I quote the poem as it appears in the 1609 (though all italics are Mahood's) quarto and follow it by her comment:

> When to the Sessions of sweet silent thought,
> I sommon vp remembrance of things past,
> I sigh the lacke of many a thing I sought,
> And with the old woes new waile my *deare* times waste:
> Then can I drowne an eye (vn-vs'd to flow)
> For *precious* friends hid in deaths dateles night,
> And weepe a fresh loues long since *canceld* woe,
> And mone th'*expence* of many a vannisht sight.
> Then can I greeue at greeuances *fore-gon*,
> And heauily from woe to woe *tell* ore
> The sad *account* of fore-bemoned mone,
> Which I new *pay* as if not *payd* before.
>   But if the while I thinke on thee (*deare* friend)
>   All losses are restord, and sorrowes end.

Sweet sets the tone of this in the first line. Shakespeare's melancholy is well-savoured. 'Summon' suggests that he is too judiciously detached from his memories for them to be painful to him, and this detachment is implicit in *dear, precious, cancelled, expense, tell, account, pay*. Besides their strongly felt meanings, these words all have neutral meanings which are as impersonal as book-keeping entries; *expense*, for example, means primarily 'the price paid', whereas in 'Th'expence of spirit' this meaning is subordinate to the emotive one. Even when an emotion is stated, the tone of the verse dissipates the force of the statement. 'Then can I greeue at greeuances fore-gon' has the suggestion of 'I could upset myself – if I tried'; the verbal jingle robs the line of any solemnity, and grievances *foregone* are repudiated and forgotten as well as simply past. This is not the anguish of Francesca over past happiness in days of misery, but the contemplation of old misfortunes in a happy time. Shakespeare's eye, in fact, is kept on the credit side of the ledger all through the poem, and when the *dear* friend is produced at the last we understand why this reverie over disaster has been far more sweet than bitter.

Like much academic criticism of the last forty or fifty years this admirably respects the particularity of the sonnets, but it is unusual in its concern for the poems' artistic wholeness, as an issue directly faced. More often scholars set out to illustrate Shakespeare's originality, which is not at all the same thing. And yet affirmations of originality when made boldly enough amount to claims for artistic achievement as well. This is, for example, the case with F. T. Prince's essay of 1960, 'The Sonnet from Wyatt to Shakespeare'. Here the sonnets are looked at in the context of their predecessors in English literature and the conclusion is as follows:

> A new moral sensibility, a new kind of devotion (and a singularly gratuitous one), are wrought out in the Sonnets. There were no conventions, no precedents in the tradition of love-poetry, for the central reality of Shakespeare's passion. Such conventions he takes up – for example, sonnets on absence, on going a journey, on not being able to sleep or sonnets promising immortality through poetry ... – are almost negligible in their context. For one thing, they are used with the force and freedom of Shakespeare's personal rhetoric, and consequently transformed. For another, they are usually conventions of mere circumstance or occasion or

expression, dramatic setting for an emotion which they project, but do not interpret.

It is striking how many of those who have commented well on the sonnets have, like Professor Prince, also been poets – Crowe Ransom and Empson, for example. W. H. Auden too has a wide-ranging if rather straggling essay on the poems, originally the introduction to the Signet Shakespeare edition of them (1964). Perhaps the most interesting aspect of Auden's essay is his treatment of the poet's relation with his friend. He maintains that at the heart of the sonnets rests a 'natural mystical experience' which he describes as 'the Vision of Eros':

The Vision of Eros ... is concerned with a single person, who is revealed to the subject as being of infinite sacred importance. The classic descriptions of it are to be found in Plato's *Symposium*, Dante's *La Vita Nuova*, and some of these sonnets by Shakespeare.

It can, it seems, be experienced before puberty. If it occurs later, though the subject is aware of its erotic nature, his own desire is always completely subordinate to the sacredness of the beloved person who is felt to be infinitely superior to the lover. Before anything else, the lover desires the happiness of the beloved.

The Vision of Eros is probably a much rarer experience than most people in our culture suppose, but, when it is genuine, I do not think it makes any sense to apply to it terms like heterosexual or homosexual. Such terms can only be legitimately applied to the profane erotic experiences with which we are all familiar, to lust, for example, an interest in another solely as a sexual object, and that combination of sexual desire and *philia*, affection based upon mutual interests, values, and shared experiences which is the securest basis for a happy marriage.

That, in the Vision of Eros, the erotic is the medium, not the cause, is proved, I think, by the fact, on which all who have written about it with authority agree, that it cannot long survive an actual sexual relationship. Indeed, it is very doubtful if the Vision can ever be mutual: the story of Tristan and Isolde is a myth, not an instance of what can historically occur. To be receptive to it, it would seem that the subject must be exceptionally imaginative. Class feelings also seem to play a role; no one, apparently, can have such a vision about an individual who belongs to a social group which he has been brought up to regard as inferior to his own, so that its members are not, for him, fully persons.

The medium of the Vision is, however, undoubtedly erotic. Nobody who was unconscious of an erotic interest on his part would use the frank, if not brutal, sexual image which Shakespeare employs in speaking of his friend's exclusive interest in women.

> But since she pricked thee out for women's pleasure,
> Mine be thy love, and thy love's use their treasure.
>
> (20)

The beloved is always beautiful in the impersonal sense of the word as well as the personal.

The Petrarchan distinction, employed by Shakespeare in a number of his sonnets, between the love of the eye and the love of the heart, is an attempt, I think, to express the difference between these two kinds of beauty and our response to them.

In the Vision of Eros, both are always present. But, to the lover, the second is the more important. Dante certainly thought that Beatrice was a girl whose beauty everybody would admire, but it wouldn't have entered his head to compare her for beauty with other Florentine girls of the same age. [. . .]

It is consistent with Shakespeare's cast of mind as we meet it in the plays, where it is impossible to be certain what his personal beliefs were on any subject, that the sonnets should contain no theory of love: Shakespeare contents himself with simply describing the experience.

Though the primary experience from which they started was, I believe, the Vision of Eros, that is, of course, not all they are about. For the vision to remain undimmed, it is probably necessary that the lover have very little contact with the beloved, however nice a person she (or he) may be. Dante, after all, only saw Beatrice once or twice, and she probably knew little about him. The story of the sonnets seems to me to be the story of an agonized struggle by Shakespeare to preserve the glory of the vision he had been granted in a relationship, lasting at least three years, with a person who seemed intent by his actions upon covering the vision with dirt.

As outsiders, the impression we get of his friend is one of a young man who was not really very nice, very conscious of his good looks, able to switch on the charm at any moment, but essentially frivolous, cold-hearted, and self-centred, aware, probably, that he had some power over Shakespeare – if he thought about it at all, no doubt he gave it a cynical explanation – but with no conception of the intensity of the feelings he had, unwittingly, aroused. Somebody, in fact, rather like Bassanio in *The Merchant of Venice*.

Joseph Pequigney, whose *Such is My Love* (1985) sets forth a very detailed and a scholarly case for reading the sonnets as an account of a homosexual relationship, naturally takes exception to Auden's sublimation of sexuality in this account of the Vision of Eros, and indeed is shocked by it. Perhaps it would be wise to let Pequigney himself express some of his objections to other views on the sexuality of the sonnets which tend to downplay the homoerotic element:

Some few scholars and critics, from G. Wilson Knight in 1955 to Kenneth Muir in 1979, do discern a homoerotic response of sorts in the Shakespearean sonneteer.

Knight terms this response 'homosexual idealism', by which he means that it is a 'strong sexual impulse' wholly divorced from 'physical vice' or carnal enactment, or a 'fine physical ardour' that is 'less a matter of desire than of adoration'. (As to 'desire', let 45.3, 51.9–10, and 57.2 set the record straight.) An impulse without an outlet, without, even, sublimation, may be the formula for frustration, but Knight can 'somehow feel' that the 'love is grander and more perfect' in this condition. C. S. Lewis argues against 'pederasty' on the curious grounds that 'Shakespeare, and indeed Shakespeare's age, did nothing by halves', and if he had intended to be 'the poet of pederasty, I think he would have left us in no doubt'. I think that he left us in none. Yet Lewis has a point, if one that again goes contrary to his intention: the poet is homoerotic not by halves but in both desire and its gratification. But Knight's Shakespeare does go halfway: he feels the sexual impulse but is inhibited from acting on it.

A major difficulty with the critical readings that concede the poet's response to the friend to be erotic is that the concession makes so little difference. Kenneth Muir can write, concerning Sonnet 20, that 'the Poet recognizes frankly that his love is erotic as well as spiritual'. He quickly adds, 'yet there seems to be no thought in his mind of the possibility of a physical consummation of his love, or *even that he would have been tempted if the possibility had existed*'. In what way, then, is the love *erotic*? This brief affirmation of its being so is the sum and substance of what Muir's book-length study has to offer on the subject. The exposition proceeds without further elaboration, and excision of the statement would change next to nothing. If Muir had chosen to deny eroticism of the love, only a sentence or two would have to be modified, and the illogicality could then be excised. Some other critics may devote a bit more space to discussing the postulated eroticism, but the results are much the same: it does not affect the poet's conduct, and it has a negligible effect, if any, on their readings of the sonnets.

There is some force in what Pequigney says, though in my introduction I try to explain why his argument fails in the end to establish itself as superior to Auden's. Doubtless, much more will be made in the future of the issue of sexuality in the sonnets. But does the excellence of these poems hinge on the outcome of that issue? Auden, by placing Shakespeare in the company of Plato and Dante certainly values him for his rendering of the Vision of Eros: equally clearly, a vision is a vision is a vision. To label an attitude, or point of view or way of seeing, a 'vision' is to some extent to put it beyond criticism.

The most influential work on the sonnets in the second half of the twentieth century has probably been Stephen Booth's *Essay on Shakespeare's Sonnets* (1969). This is a work in the tradition of detailed exegesis initiated by Graves and Riding, concentrating on the co-existence within the sonnets of conflicting systems of organization, formal, logical, ideological, syntactic, rhythmic and phonetic. Booth is particularly good on the way in which sonnets relate to their predecessors and their successors, in effect vindicating the often challenged ordering of the sonnets in the 1609 Quarto. Booth went on to produce an edition (1977) where commentary provides an exhaustive and exhausting account of ambiguities and double meanings in the sonnets. Indeed, so extensive is the commentary that it may seem to call in question Booth's earlier final assessment of the sonnets in his *Essay*:

> The many different patterns that exist in any sonnet by virtue of its form make it seem crowded or, if that word has irremediably derisive connotations, full. Shakespeare's enlargement of the number and kinds of patterns makes his sonnets seem full to bursting not only with the quantity of different actions but with the energy generated from their conflict. The reader has constantly to cope with the multitudinous organizations of a Shakespeare

sonnet; he is engaged and active. Nonetheless, the sonnets are above all else artificial, humanly ordered; the reader is always capable of coping. He always has the comfort and security of a frame of reference, but the frames of reference are not constant, and their number seems limitless.

The solace to be found in a Shakespeare sonnet is brief indeed, but it is as great a solace as literature can give – the feeling that the weight of liberty is not too much. That is a remarkable achievement for a reader and for the writer who gives it to him. I think it is that achievement which readers acknowledge when they praise Shakespeare's sonnets.

The judgment is in some ways persuasive, and yet it is odd that in talking about these poems, Booth should mention liberty without reference to the love that is their subject-matter. That must be the sign of more still to be said.

One thing more might, for example, have been said about 'A Lover's Complaint', which is significantly absent from his account, as from that of earlier writers. It is only very recently that the poem has been viewed as one related to the other sonnets and as almost certainly Shakespearean, so that the lack of appreciative comment is perhaps unsurprising. And yet it is a poem whose context is authentically Shakespearean, and however unpolished its phrasing it is still memorable – vastly more so, one might think, than many a better known poem of complaint. Its literary antecedents and its teasing nature have been expounded at length by John Kerrigan in his *Motives of Woe* (1991) with learning and subtlety but without the *panache* needed to establish it firmly in readers' affections. 'A Lover's Complaint' has yet to have its day.

INDEX OF FIRST LINES

ACKNOWLEDGEMENTS

I should like to thank Katherine Duncan-Jones for many enjoyable and instructive conversations on the subject of these poems. She has improved my understanding of them enormously and her own edition for the New Arden Shakespeare will be a necessary port of reference in the future. She is responsible for none of the shortcomings of this edition.

The editor and publishers wish to thank the following for permission to use copyright material:

Board of Literary Management of the late Laura (Riding) Jackson and Carcanet Press on behalf of the Estate of Robert Graves for an extract from Laura Riding and Robert Graves, *A Survey of Modernist Poetry* (1927);

Faber & Faber Ltd for an extract from W. H. Auden, 'Shakespeare's Sonnets' (1964) from *Forewords and Afterwords*, ed. Edward Mendelson.

Every effort has been made to trace all the copyright holders but if any have been inadvertently overlooked the publishers will be pleased to make the necessary arrangement at the first opportunity.

THE EVERYMAN SHAKESPEARE
EDITED BY JOHN F. ANDREWS

The Everyman Shakespeare is the most comprehensive, up-to-date paperback edition of the plays and poems, featuring:

• face-to-face text and notes

• a chronology of Shakespeare's life and times

• a rich selection of critical and theatrical responses to the play over the centuries

• foreword by an actor or director describing the play in performance

• up-to-date commentary on the play

ALREADY PUBLISHED

The Merchant of Venice	£2.99
Romeo and Juliet	£2.99
Macbeth	£2.99
A Midsummer Night's Dream	£2.99

MARCH

Antony and Cleopatra	£3.99
Hamlet	£2.99

JUNE

Measure for Measure	£2.99
The Tempest	£2.99

AUGUST

Othello	£2.99
Twelfth Night	£2.99

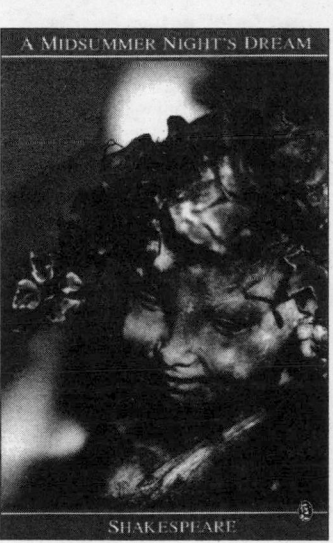

£2.99

POETRY IN EVERYMAN

A SELECTION

Silver Poets of the Sixteenth Century

EDITED BY

DOUGLAS BROOKS-DAVIES
A new edition of this famous Everyman collection **£6.99**

Complete Poems

JOHN DONNE
The father of metaphysical verse in this highly-acclaimed edition **£6.99**

Complete English Poems, Of Education, Areopagitica

JOHN MILTON
An excellent introduction to Milton's poetry and prose **£6.99**

Selected Poems

JOHN DRYDEN
A poet's portrait of Restoration England **£4.99**

Selected Poems and Prose

PERCY BYSSHE SHELLEY
'The essential Shelley' in one volume **£3.50**

Women Romantic Poets 1780-1830: An Anthology

Hidden talent from the Romantic era rediscovered **£5.99**

Poems in Scots and English

ROBERT BURNS
The best of Scotland's greatest lyric poet **£4.99**

Selected Poems

D. H. LAWRENCE
A new, authoritative selection spanning the whole of Lawrence's literary career **£4.99**

The Poems

W. B. YEATS
Ireland's greatest lyric poet surveyed in this ground-breaking edition **£7.99**

£5.99

AVAILABILITY

All books are available from your local bookshop or direct from
Littlehampton Book Services Cash Sales, 14 Eldon Way, Lineside Estate, Littlehampton, West Sussex BN17 7HE. PRICES ARE SUBJECT TO CHANGE.

To order any of the books, please enclose a cheque (in £ sterling) made payable to Littlehampton Book Services, or phone your order through with credit card details (Access, Visa or Mastercard) on 0903 721596 (24 hour answering service) stating card number and expiry date. Please add £1.25 for package and postage to the total value of your order.

In the USA, for further information and a complete catalogue call 1-800-526-2778.